January 1987

To Alison, on becoming
a Junior Soldier —
with love from
Auntie Ida

Good News from the Psalms

In Colour

Today's English Version

The Bible Societies

Produced by Creative Publishing, Northwood, Middlesex.
Published 1986 by Bible Society. Permission to reproduce any part of this publication should be requested from Bible Society, Stonehill Green, Westlea,
Swindon, Wiltshire SN5 7DG.
British usage text first published by The Bible Societies and Collins 1976.
Bible text © American Bible Society, New York 1970, 1976.
Colour photography © Creative Publishing, Northwood, Middx.
Bible Society ISBN 0 564 05001 6   TEV 563 PC

Special thanks to those who have been involved in the production of this edition.
Photographers A. Bedding, P. Brice, R. Chouler, A. Hayward, R. Heywood, R.F.Hicks, J. Hicks, D. Leighton, P. Marsh, D. Parker, B. Pont, D. Skinner,
D. Townsend, S. Zisman.
Design and layout R. Backhouse, R. Chouler, P. Hicks, A. Hicks.
Typesetting Creative Editors & Writers Ltd.
Picture Research J. Belben, P. Hicks, S. Mills.
Colour originated and printed in Hong Kong by Mandarin Offset Marketing (HK) Ltd.

Bible Societies exist to provide resources for Bible distribution and use. Bible Society in England and Wales (BFBS) is a member of the United Bible
Societies, an international partnership working in over 150 countries. Their common aim is to reach all people with the Bible, or some part of it, in a
language they can understand and at a price they can afford. Parts of the Bible have now been translated into approximately 1,800 languages. Bible
Societies aim to help every church at every point where it uses the Bible. You are invited to share in this work by your prayers and gifts. Bible Society in
your country will be very happy to provide details of its activity.

THE BOOK OF PSALMS is the hymnbook and prayer book of the Bible. Composed by different authors over a long period of time, these hymns and prayers were collected and used by the people of Israel in their worship, and eventually this collection was included in their Holy Scriptures.

These religious poems are of many kinds: there are hymns of praise and worship of God; prayers for help, protection, and salvation; pleas for forgiveness; songs of thanksgiving for God's blessings; and petitions for the punishment of enemies. These prayers are personal and national; some portray the most intimate feelings of one person, while others represent the needs and feelings of all the people of God.

Many of the Psalms are quoted in the New Testament, and such passages as Mary's song of praise (Luke 1.46–55), Zechariah's prophecy (Luke 1.68–79), and Simeon's prayer of thanksgiving (Luke 2.29–32) reflect the language and style of the psalms. They were used by Jesus, quoted by the writers of the New Testament, and became the treasured book of worship of the Christian Church from its very beginning.

This translation of the Psalms attempts to represent the meaning of the Hebrew text as faithfully as possible, and at the same time convey something of the grace and beauty of the original poetry. The basic poetic structure of the Psalms consists of a statement which is repeated, in a modified fashion, in the next line. Sometimes this parallelism is continued over several lines. The possible variations are almost unlimited, and the reader who is aware of them will discover new beauty in the Psalms. In addition, unusual words and figurative expressions help create and sustain a poetic atmosphere.

Ancient Hebrew poetry did not have rhyme, and the metre was quite different from what is commonly used in English. This translation has been made in free verse, and the translators have tried to put the Psalms in easy-flowing, rhythmical lines that can be effective in public worship as well as in private devotion.

Today's English Version is a distinctively new translation, which does not conform to traditional vocabulary or style. It seeks instead to express the meaning of the Hebrew text in words and forms accepted as standard by people everywhere who employ English as a means of communication.

Where there is general agreement that the Hebrew text presents unresolved difficulties in interpretation, this translation employs the evidence of other ancient texts or follows present-day scholarly consensus.

The Bible in Today's English Version is called the *Good News Bible* and is available from Bible Society and all good bookshops.

It has been said that, while the rest of the Bible speaks *to* us the Psalms speak *for* us. They give us words for many different occasions, moods and needs. Indeed, some psalms cover within their lines a whole range of human experience and emotion. The following list will help you find those psalms that are most appropriate to your present circumstances.

PRAISING GOD

To God our King
  Psalms 24; 47; 93; 96; 97; 99
To God who loves and cares for us
  Psalms 103; 107; 113; 116; 117; 145; 146
To God our Creator
  Psalms 8; 19; 29; 104; 147; 148
To God our judge
  Psalms 33; 75; 76; 82; 97; 99
To God who is faithful
  Psalms 100; 103; 111; 145
To God who knows us
  Psalms 8; 139
To God our helper
  Psalms 105; 121; 124; 138
To God who gives us what we need
  Psalms 16; 23; 65; 67; 111; 147
To God who is merciful
  Psalms 107; 113; 116
To God who protects us
  Psalms 18; 34; 46; 91; 115; 124
To God who never changes
  Psalms 103; 125; 138; 139
To God, the Lord of history
  Psalms 78; 105; 106

ENCOURAGEMENT

To trust God
  Psalms 11; 13; 16; 23; 31; 37; 40; 62; 131
To worship God
  Psalms 24; 84; 95; 96; 98; 100; 134; 147; 150
To obey God
  Psalms 15; 33; 34; 95; 128
To seek forgiveness
  Psalms 25; 32; 51; 130
To have faith in God
  Psalms 46; 62; 146
To live a good life
  Psalms 1; 15; 26; 34; 36; 37; 92; 112; 119.1–8; 128; 131

To tell others about God
Psalms 9; 34; 40; 51; 92; 107; 116; 118
To pray for your nation
(These are prayers for God's people in the Old Testament—the nation of Israel)
Psalms 79; 80; 85
To depend on God
Psalms 16; 62; 118; 123
To hear and obey God's Word
Psalms 19; 78.1–8; 119.1–24, 33–80, 97–144

FOR SPECIAL TIMES

In the morning
Psalms 5; 90
At night
Psalms 3; 4; 17; 30; 63; 130; 141
When you are young
Psalms 34; 119.1–16
At the end of life
Psalms 37; 71; 121
For a wedding
Psalm 45
When you long for God's presence
Psalms 42; 63; 84; 130; 143
In sickness or suffering
Psalms 9; 13; 22; 38
When you need guidance
Psalms 25; 27
When you are anxious
Psalms 25; 77; 116
In the battle between good and evil
Psalms 12; 14; 37; 49; 94
When suffering injustice
Psalms 7; 26; 35; 119.73–88
When prayers seem unanswered
Psalms 10; 13
When you are depressed
Psalms 6; 23; 34; 42; 43; 130; 143
When you need to know God's forgiveness
Psalms 25; 51
In times of trouble
Psalms 6; 22; 31; 34; 40; 142
When you are afraid
Psalms 27; 46; 56
When friends betray you
Psalm 55
When you feel overwhelmed
Psalms 6; 138
When you face enemies
Psalms 12; 17; 64

READ ALL THE PSALMS IN SIX MONTHS

This reading plan takes you through all of the 150 psalms in six months. Each day you are given a psalm, or part of a psalm for the longer psalms. The 176 verses of Psalm 119 have been divided into their natural sections which make 21 days of readings. The headings from the Good News translation of the Psalms are given as titles for each day's reading. The variety of subjects mentioned in the Psalms, as well as the Psalmist's trust in the Lord God, will become apparent as you read through all the Psalms in the course of six months.

1st Month

BOOK ONE
(Psalms 1–41))

DAY	PSALM	TITLE	TICK
1	1	True Happiness	✓
2	2	God's Chosen King	✓
3	3	Morning Prayer for Help	✓
4	4	Evening Prayer for Help	✓
5	5	A Prayer for Protection	✓
6	6	A Prayer for Help in Time of Trouble	✓
7	7	A Prayer for Justice	✓
8	8	God's Glory and Man's Dignity	✓
9	9	Thanksgiving to God for His Justice	✓
10	10	A Prayer for Justice	✓
11	11	Confidence in the LORD	✓
12	12	A Prayer for Help	✓
13	13	A Prayer for Help	✓
14	14	The Wickedness of Men	✓
15	15	What God Requires	✓
16	16	A Prayer of Confidence	✓
17	17	The Prayer of an Innocent Man	✓
18	18.1–19	David's Song of Victory	✓
19	18.20–34	David's Song of Victory—cont.	✓
20	18.35–50	David's Song of Victory—cont.	✓
21	19.1–6	God's Glory in Creation	✓
22	19.7–14	The Law of the LORD	✓
23	20	A Prayer for Victory	✓
24	21	Praise for Victory	✓
25	22	A Cry of Anguish and a Song of Praise	✓
26	23	The LORD Our Shepherd	✓
27	24	The Great King	✓
28	25	A Prayer for Guidance and Protection	✓
29	26	The Prayer of a Good Man	✓
30	27	A Prayer of Praise	✓

2nd Month

DAY	PSALM	TITLE	TICK
1	28	A Prayer for Help	✓
2	29	The Voice of the LORD in the Storm	✓
3	30	A Prayer of Thanksgiving	✓
4	31	A Prayer of Trust in God	✓
5	32	Confession and Forgiveness	✓
6	33	A Song of Praise	✓
7	34	In Praise of God's Goodness	✓
8	35	A Prayer for Help	✓
9	36	The Wickedness of Man	✓
10	37.1–22	The Destiny of the Wicked and of the Good	✓
11	37.23–40	The Destiny of the Wicked and of the Good—cont.	✓

DAY	PSALM	TITLE	TICK
12	38	The Prayer of a Suffering Man	✓
13	39	The Confession of a Suffering Man	✓
14	40.1–11	A Song of Praise	✓
15	40.12–17	A Prayer for Help	✓
16	41	The Prayer of a Sick Man	✓

BOOK TWO
(Psalms 42–72)

17	42	The Prayer of a Man in Exile	✓
18	43	The Prayer of a Man in Exile	✓
19	44	A Prayer for Protection	✓
20	45	A Royal Wedding Song	✓
21	46	God Is with Us	✓
22	47	The Supreme Ruler	✓
23	48	Zion, the City of God	✓
24	49	The Foolishness of Trusting in Riches	✓
25	50	True Worship	✓
26	51	A Prayer for Forgiveness	✓
27	52	God's Judgement and Grace	✓
28	53	The Wickedness of Men	✓
29	54	A Prayer for Protection from Enemies	✓
30	55	The Prayer of a Man Betrayed by a Friend	✓

3rd Month

DAY	PSALM	TITLE	TICK
1	56	A Prayer of Trust in God	✓
2	57	A Prayer for Help	✓
3	58	A Prayer for God to Punish the Wicked	✓
4	59	A Prayer for Safety	✓
5	60	A Prayer for Deliverance	✓
6	61	A Prayer for Protection	✓
7	62	Confidence in God's Protection	✓
8	63	Longing for God	✓
9	64	A Prayer for Protection	✓
10	65	Praise and Thanksgiving	✓
11	66	A Song of Praise and Thanksgiving	✓
12	67	A Song of Thanksgiving	✓
13	68.1–18	A National Song of Triumph	✓
14	68.19–35	A National Song of Triumph—cont.	✓
15	69.1–18	A Cry for Help	✓
16	69.19–36	A Cry for Help—cont., and	
	70	A Prayer for Help	✓
17	71	An Old Man's Prayer	✓
18	72	A Prayer for the King	✓

BOOK THREE
(Psalms 73–89)

19	73	The Justice of God	✓
20	74	A Prayer for National Deliverance	✓
21	75	God the Judge	✓

DAY	PSALM	TITLE	TICK
22	76	God the Victor	☑
23	77	Comfort in Time of Distress	☑
24	78.1–20	God and His People	☑
25	78.21–39	God and His People—*cont.*	☑
26	78.40–55	God and His People—*cont.*	☑
27	78.56–72	God and His People—*cont.*	☑
28	79	A Prayer for the Nation's Deliverance	☑
29	80	A Prayer for the Nation's Restoration	☑
30	81	A Song for a Festival	☑

4th Month

DAY	PSALM	TITLE	TICK
1	82	God the Supreme Ruler	☑
2	83	A Prayer for the Defeat of Israel's Enemies	☑
3	84	Longing for God's House	☑
4	85	A Prayer for the Nation's Welfare	☑
5	86	A Prayer for Help	☑
6	87	In Praise of Jerusalem	☑
7	88	A Cry for Help	☑
8	89.1–18	A Hymn in Time of National Trouble	☑
9	89.19–37	God's Promise to David	☑
10	89.38–45	Lament over the Defeat of the King	☑
11	89.46–52	A Prayer for Deliverance	☑

BOOK FOUR
(Psalms 90–106)

DAY	PSALM	TITLE	TICK
12	90	Of God and Man	☑
13	91	God Our Protector	☑
14	92	A Song of Praise *and*	
	93	God the King	☑
15	94	God the Judge of All	☑
16	95	A Song of Praise	☑
17	96	God the Supreme King	☑
18	97	God the Supreme Ruler	☑
19	98	God the Ruler of the World	
20	99	God the Supreme King	☑
21	100	A Hymn of Praise *and*	
	101	A King's Promise	☑
22	102	The Prayer of a Troubled Young Man	☑
23	103	The Love of God	☑
24	104.1–23	In Praise of the Creator	☑
25	104.24–35	In Praise of the Creator—*cont.*	☑
26	105.1–25	God and His People	☑
27	105.26–45	God and His People—*cont.*	☑
28	106.1–15	The LORD's Goodness to His People	☑
29	106.16–33	The LORD's Goodness to His People —*cont.*	☑
30	106.34–48	The LORD's Goodness to His People —*cont.*	☑

5th Month

BOOK FIVE
(Psalms 107–150)

DAY	PSALM	TITLE	TICK
1	107.1–16	In Praise of God's Goodness	☑
2	107.17–32	In Praise of God's Goodness—*cont.*	☑
3	107.33–43	In Praise of God's Goodness—*cont.*	☑
4	108	A Prayer for Help against Enemies	☑
5	109	The Complaint of a Man in Trouble	☑
6	110	The LORD and His Chosen King	☑
7	111	In Praise of the LORD	☑
8	112	The Happiness of a Good Person	☑
9	113	In Praise of the LORD's Goodness	☑
10	114	A Passover Song	☑
11	115	The One True God	☑
12	116 & 117	Praising God	☐
13	118	A Prayer of Thanks for Victory	☐
14	119.1–8	The Law of the LORD	☐
15	119.9–16	Obedience to the Law of the LORD	☐
16	119.17–24	Happiness in the Law of the LORD	☐
17	119.25–32	Determination to Obey the Law of the LORD	
18	119.33–40	A Prayer for Understanding	
19	119.41–48	Trusting the Law of the LORD	
20	119.49–56	Confidence in the Law of the LORD	
21	119.57–64	Devotion to the Law of the LORD	
22	119.65–72	The Value of the Law of the LORD	
23	119.73–80	The Justice of the Law of the LORD	
24	119.81–88	A Prayer for Deliverance	
25	119.89–96	Faith in the Law of the LORD	
26	119.97–104	Love for the Law of the LORD	
27	119.105–112	Light from the Law of the LORD	
28	119.113–120	Safety in the Law of the LORD	
29	119.121–128	Obedience to the Law of the LORD	
30	119.129–136	Desire to Obey the Law of the LORD	☐

6th Month

DAY	PSALM	TITLE	TICK
1	119.137–144	The Justice of the Law of the LORD	☐
2	119.145–152	A Prayer for Deliverance	☐
3	119.153–160	A Plea for Help	☐
4	119.161–168	Dedication to the Law of the LORD	☐
5	119.169–176	A Prayer for Help	☐
6	120 & 121	The LORD Our Helper and Protector	☐
7	122	In Praise of Jerusalem	☐
8	123 & 124	Prayers for Mercy and Protection	☐
9	125 & 126	God gives Security and Deliverance	☐
10	127 & 128	God's Goodness and Man's Obedience	☐
11	129	A Prayer against Israel's Enemies	☐
12	130 & 131	Humble Trust in God's Help	☐
13	132	In Praise of the Temple	☐
14	133 & 134	Brotherly Love *and* Praise to God	☐
15	135	A Hymn of Praise	☐
16	136	A Hymn of Thanksgiving	☐
17	137	A Lament of Israelites in Exile	☐
18	138	A Prayer of Thanksgiving	☐
19	139	God's Complete Knowledge and Care	☐
20	140	A Prayer for Protection	☐
21	141	An Evening Prayer	☐
22	142	A Prayer for Help	☐
23	143	A Prayer for Help	☐
24	144	A King Thanks God for Victory	☐
25	145	A Hymn of Praise	☐
26	146	In Praise of God the Saviour	☐
27	147	In Praise of God the Almighty	☐
28	148	A Call for the Universe to Praise God	☐
29	149	A Hymn of Praise	☐
30	150	Praise the LORD!	☐

THE
PSALMS

INTRODUCTION

The book of *Psalms* is the hymn book and prayer book of the Bible. Composed by different authors over a long period of time, these hymns and prayers were collected and used by the people of Israel in their worship, and eventually this collection was included in their Scriptures.

These religious poems are of many kinds: there are hymns of praise and worship of God; prayers for help, protection, and salvation; pleas for forgiveness; songs of thanksgiving for God's blessings; and petitions for the punishment of enemies. These prayers are both personal and national; some portray the most intimate feelings of one person, while others represent the needs and feelings of all the people of God.

The psalms were used by Jesus, quoted by the writers of the New Testament, and became the treasured book of worship of the Christian Church from its beginning.

Outline of Contents
The 150 psalms are grouped into five collections,
or books, as follows:

Psalms 1—41
Psalms 42—72
Psalms 73—89
Psalms 90—106
Psalms 107—150

BOOK ONE
(Psalms 1—41)

True Happiness

1 Happy are those
who reject the advice of evil men,
who do not follow the example of sinners
or join those who have no use for God.
² Instead, they find joy in obeying the Law of the LORD,
and they study it day and night.

³ They are like trees that grow beside a stream,
that bear fruit at the right time,
and whose leaves do not dry up.
They succeed in everything they do.

⁴ But evil men are not like this at all;
they are like straw that the wind blows away.
⁵ Sinners will be condemned by God
and kept apart from God's own people.
⁶ The righteous are guided and protected by the LORD,
but the evil are on the way to their doom.

God's Chosen King

2 Why do the nations plan rebellion?
Why do people make their useless
plots?
2Their kings revolt,
their rulers plot together against the LORD
and against the king he chose.
3'Let us free ourselves from their rule,' they
say;
'let us throw off their control.'

4From his throne in heaven the Lord laughs
and mocks their feeble plans.
5Then he warns them in anger
and terrifies them with his fury.
6'On Zion, my sacred hill,' he says,
'I have installed my king.'

7'I will announce,' says the king, 'what the
LORD has declared.
He said to me: "You are my son;
today I have become your father.
8Ask, and I will give you all the nations;
the whole earth will be yours.
9You will break them with an iron rod;
you will shatter them in pieces like a clay
pot."'

10Now listen to this warning, you kings;
learn this lesson, you rulers of the world:
11Serve the LORD with fear;
12   tremble and bow down to him;
or else his anger will be quickly aroused,
and you will suddenly die.
Happy are all who go to him for protection.

Morning Prayer for Help

3 I have so many enemies, LORD,
so many who turn against me!
2They talk about me and say,
'God will not help him.'

3But you, O LORD, are always my shield from
danger;
you give me victory
and restore my courage.
4I call to the LORD for help,
and from his sacred hill he answers me.

5I lie down and sleep,

and all night long the LORD protects me.
6I am not afraid of the thousands of enemies
who surround me on every side.

7Come, LORD! Save me, my God!
You punish all my enemies
and leave them powerless to harm me.

... you, O LORD, are always my shield...

8Victory comes from the LORD—
may he bless his people.

Evening Prayer for Help

4 Answer me when I pray,
O God, my defender!
When I was in trouble, you helped me.
Be kind to me now and hear my prayer.

2How long will you people insult me?
How long will you love what is worthless
and go after what is false?

3Remember that the LORD has chosen the
righteous for his own,
and he hears me when I call to him.

4Tremble with fear and stop sinning;
think deeply about this,
when you lie in silence on your beds.
5Offer the right sacrifices to the LORD,
and put your trust in him.

6There are many who pray:
'Give us more blessings, O LORD.
Look on us with kindness!'

**You alone, O LORD,
keep me perfectly safe.**

7But the joy that you have given me
is more than they will ever have
with all their corn and wine.

8When I lie down, I go to sleep in peace;
you alone, O LORD, keep me perfectly safe.

A Prayer for Protection

5 Listen to my words, O LORD,
and hear my sighs.
[2]Listen to my cry for help,
my God and king!

I pray to you, O LORD;
[3]   you hear my voice in the morning;
at sunrise I offer my prayer
and wait for your answer.

[4]You are not a God who is pleased with
wrongdoing;
you allow no evil in your presence.
[5]You cannot stand the sight of proud men;
you hate all wicked people.
[6]You destroy all liars
and despise violent, deceitful men.

[7]But because of your great love
I can come into your house;
I can worship in your holy Temple
and bow down to you in reverence.

[8]LORD, I have so many enemies!
Lead me to do your will;
make your way plain for me to follow.

[9]What my enemies say can never be trusted;
they only want to destroy.

**Lead me to do your will;
make your way plain for me to follow.**

Their words are flattering and smooth,
but full of deadly deceit.
[10]Condemn and punish them, O God;
may their own plots cause their ruin.
Drive them out of your presence
because of their many sins
and their rebellion against you.

[11]But all who find safety in you will rejoice;
they can always sing for joy.
Protect those who love you;

because of you they are truly happy.
¹²You bless those who obey you, LORD;
your love protects them like a shield.

A Prayer for Help in Time of Trouble

6 LORD, don't be angry and rebuke me!
Don't punish me in your anger!
²I am worn out, O LORD; have pity on
me!
Give me strength; I am completely
exhausted
³ and my whole being is deeply troubled.
How long, O LORD, will you wait to help me?

⁴Come and save me, LORD;
in your mercy rescue me from death.
⁵In the world of the dead you are not
remembered;
no one can praise you there.

⁶I am worn out with grief;
every night my bed is damp from my
weeping;
my pillow is soaked with tears.
⁷I can hardly see;
my eyes are so swollen
from the weeping caused by my enemies.

⁸Keep away from me, you evil men!
The LORD hears my weeping;
⁹ he listens to my cry for help
and will answer my prayer.

The LORD hears my weeping.

---

¹⁰My enemies will know the bitter shame of
defeat;
in sudden confusion they will be driven
away.

A Prayer for Justice

7 O LORD, my God, I come to you for
protection;
rescue me and save me from all who
pursue me,
²or else like a lion they will carry me off
where no one can save me,
and there they will tear me to pieces.

³⁻⁴O LORD, my God, if I have wronged anyone,
if I have betrayed a friend
or without cause done violence to my
enemy—
if I have done any of these things—
⁵then let my enemies pursue me and catch
me,
let them cut me down and kill me
and leave me lifeless on the ground!

⁶Rise in your anger, O LORD!
Stand up against the fury of my enemies;
rouse yourself and help me!
Justice is what you demand,
⁷ so bring together all the peoples round
you,
and rule over them from above.
⁸You are the judge of all mankind.
Judge in my favour, O LORD;
you know that I am innocent.
⁹You are a righteous God
and judge our thoughts and desires.
Stop the wickedness of evil men
and reward those who are good.

¹⁰God is my protector;
he saves those who obey him.
¹¹God is a righteous judge
and always condemns the wicked.
¹²If they do not change their ways,
God will sharpen his sword.
He bends his bow and makes it ready;
¹³ he takes up his deadly weapons
and aims his burning arrows.

¹⁴See how wicked people think up evil;
they plan trouble and practise deception.
¹⁵But in the traps they set for others,
they themselves get caught.
¹⁶So they are punished by their own evil
and are hurt by their own violence.

¹⁷I thank the LORD for his justice,
I sing praises to the LORD, the Most High.

God's Glory and Man's Dignity

8 O LORD, our Lord,
your greatness is seen in all the
world!
Your praise reaches up to the heavens;

² it is sung by children and babies.
You are safe and secure from all your
enemies;
you stop anyone who opposes you.

³When I look at the sky, which you have made,
at the moon and the stars, which you set
in their places—
⁴what is man, that you think of him;
mere man, that you care for him?

⁵Yet you made him inferior only to yourself;
you crowned him with glory and honour.
⁶You appointed him ruler over everything
you made;
you placed him over all creation:

**O Lord, our Lord,
your greatness is seen
in all the world!**

⁷ sheep and cattle, and the wild animals too;
⁸ the birds and the fish
and the creatures in the seas.

⁹O Lord, our Lord,
your greatness is seen in all the world!

Thanksgiving to God for His Justice

9 I will praise you, Lord, with all my
heart;
I will tell of all the wonderful things
you have done.
²I will sing with joy because of you.
I will sing praise to you, Almighty God.

³My enemies turn back when you appear;
they fall down and die.
⁴You are fair and honest in your
judgements,
and you have judged in my favour.

⁵You have condemned the heathen
and destroyed the wicked;
they will be remembered no more.
⁶Our enemies are finished for ever;
you have destroyed their cities,
and they are completely forgotten.

'I will praise you, Lord, with all my heart.' (Psalm 9.1)

⁷But the LORD is king for ever;
    he has set up his throne for judgement.
⁸He rules the world with righteousness;
    he judges the nations with justice.

⁹The LORD is a refuge for the oppressed,
    a place of safety in times of trouble.
¹⁰Those who know you, LORD, will trust you;
    you do not abandon anyone who comes to
    you.

¹¹Sing praise to the LORD, who rules in Zion!
    Tell every nation what he has done!

**God remembers
those who suffer.**

---

¹²God remembers those who suffer;
    he does not forget their cry,
    and he punishes those who wrong them.

¹³Be merciful to me, O LORD!
    See the sufferings my enemies cause me!
  Rescue me from death, O LORD,
¹⁴   that I may stand before the people of
      Jerusalem
    and tell them all the things for which I
      praise you.
  I will rejoice because you saved me.

¹⁵The heathen have dug a pit and fallen in;
    they have been caught in their own trap.
¹⁶The LORD has revealed himself by his
      righteous judgements,
    and the wicked are trapped by their own
      deeds.

¹⁷Death is the destiny of all the wicked,
    of all those who reject God.
¹⁸The needy will not always be neglected;
    the hope of the poor will not be crushed
      for ever.

¹⁹Come, LORD! Do not let men defy you!
    Bring the heathen before you
    and pronounce judgement on them.
²⁰Make them afraid, O LORD;
    make them know that they are only
      mortal beings.

A Prayer for Justice

10 Why are you so far away, O LORD?
    Why do you hide yourself
      when we are in trouble?
²The wicked are proud and persecute the
    poor;
    catch them in the traps they have made.

³The wicked man is proud of his evil desires;
    the greedy man curses and rejects the
      LORD.
⁴A wicked man does not care about the LORD;
    in his pride he thinks that God doesn't
      matter.

⁵A wicked man succeeds in everything.
    He cannot understand God's judgements;
    he sneers at his enemies.
⁶He says to himself, 'I will never fail;
    I will never be in trouble.'
⁷His speech is filled with curses, lies, and
      threats;
    he is quick to speak hateful, evil words.

⁸He hides himself in the villages,
    waiting to murder innocent people.
  He spies on his helpless victims;
⁹   he waits in his hiding place like a lion.
  He lies in wait for the poor;
    he catches them in his trap and drags
      them away.

¹⁰The helpless victims lie crushed;
    brute strength has defeated them.

**You will hear
the cries of the oppressed
and the orphans.**

---

¹¹The wicked man says to himself, 'God
      doesn't care!
    He has closed his eyes and will never see
      me!'

¹²O LORD, punish those wicked men!
    Remember those who are suffering!
¹³How can a wicked man despise God
    and say to himself, 'He will not punish
      me'?

¹⁴But you do see; you take notice of trouble
    and suffering
  and are always ready to help.
The helpless man commits himself to you;
    you have always helped the needy.

¹⁵Break the power of wicked and evil men;
    punish them for the wrong they have done
    until they do it no more.

¹⁶The LORD is king for ever and ever.
    Those who worship other gods
    will vanish from his land.

¹⁷You will listen, O LORD, to the prayers of the
    lowly;
    you will give them courage.
¹⁸You will hear the cries of the oppressed and
    the orphans;
    you will judge in their favour,
    so that mortal men may cause terror no
    more.

Confidence in the LORD

11 I trust in the LORD for safety.
        How foolish of you to say to
        me,
'Fly away like a bird to the mountains,
² because the wicked have drawn their
    bows and aimed their arrows

to shoot from the shadows at good men.
³There is nothing a good man can do
    when everything falls apart.'

⁴The LORD is in his holy temple;
    he has his throne in heaven.
He watches people everywhere
    and knows what they are doing.

**The LORD is righteous and
loves good deeds.**

⁵He examines the good and the wicked alike;
    the lawless he hates with all his heart.

⁶He sends down flaming coals and burning
    sulphur on the wicked;
    he punishes them with scorching winds.
⁷The LORD is righteous and loves good deeds;
    those who do them will live in his
    presence.

A Prayer for Help

12 Help us, LORD!
        There is not a good man left;
        honest men can no longer be
        found.
²All of them lie to one another;

'I trust in the LORD for safety.' (Psalm 11.1)

they deceive each other with flattery.

³Silence those flattering tongues, O LORD!
 Close those boastful mouths that say,
⁴'With our words we get what we want.
 We will say what we wish,
 and no one can stop us.'

⁵'But now I will come,' says the LORD,
 'because the needy are oppressed
 and the persecuted groan in pain.
I will give them the security they long for.'

⁶The promises of the LORD can be trusted;
 they are as genuine as silver
 refined seven times in the furnace.

**The promises of the LORD
can be trusted;
they are as genuine as silver
refined seven times...**

---

⁷⁻⁸Wicked men are everywhere,
 and everyone praises what is evil.
Keep us always safe, O LORD,
 and preserve us from such people.

A Prayer for Help

13 How much longer will you forget
 me, LORD? For ever?
 How much longer will you hide
 yourself from me?
²How long must I endure trouble?
 How long will sorrow fill my heart day
 and night?
 How long will my enemies triumph over
 me?

³Look at me, O LORD my God, and answer me.
 Restore my strength; don't let me die.
⁴Don't let my enemies say, 'We have defeated
 him.'
 Don't let them gloat over my downfall.

⁵I rely on your constant love;
 I will be glad, because you will rescue me,
⁶I will sing to you, O LORD,
 because you have been good to me.

The Wickedness of Men

14 Fools say to themselves,
 There is no God.'
 They are all corrupt,
 and they have done terrible things;
 there is no one who does what is right.

²The LORD looks down from heaven at
 mankind
 to see if there are any who are wise,
 any who worship him.
³But they have all gone wrong;
 they are all equally bad.
Not one of them does what is right,
 not a single one.

⁴'Don't they know?' asks the LORD.
 'Are all these evildoers ignorant?
They live by robbing my people,
 and they never pray to me.'

⁵But then they will be terrified,
 for God is with those who obey him.
⁶Evildoers frustrate the plans of the humble
 man,
 but the LORD is his protection.

⁷How I pray that victory
 will come to Israel from Zion.
How happy the people of Israel will be
 when the LORD makes them prosperous
 again!

What God Requires

15 LORD, who may enter your
 Temple?
 Who may worship on Zion,
 your sacred hill?

²A person who obeys God in everything
 and always does what is right,
 whose words are true and sincere,
³ and who does not slander others,
 He does no wrong to his friends
 nor spreads rumours about his
 neighbours.
⁴He despises those whom God rejects,
 but honours those who obey the LORD.
He always does what he promises,
 no matter how much it may cost.

⁵He makes loans without charging interest
and cannot be bribed to testify against the
innocent.

Whoever does these things will always be
secure.

A Prayer of Confidence

16 Protect me, O God; I trust in you
for safety.
²I say to the LORD, 'You are my
Lord;
all the good things I have come from you.'

³How excellent are the LORD's faithful people!
My greatest pleasure is to be with them.

⁴Those who rush to other gods
bring many troubles on themselves.

**You, LORD, are all I have,
and you give me all I need.**

I will not take part in their sacrifices;
I will not worship their gods.

⁵You, LORD, are all I have,
and you give me all I need;
my future is in your hands.
⁶How wonderful are your gifts to me;
how good they are!

⁷I praise the LORD, because he guides me,
and in the night my conscience warns me.
⁸I am always aware of the LORD's presence;
he is near, and nothing can shake me.

⁹And so I am thankful and glad,
and I feel completely secure,
¹⁰because you protect me from the power of
death.
I have served you faithfully,
and you will not abandon me to the world
of the dead.

¹¹You will show me the path that leads to life;
your presence fills me with joy
and brings me pleasure for ever.

The Prayer of an Innocent Man

17 Listen, O LORD, to my plea for
justice;
pay attention to my cry for
help!
Listen to my honest prayer.
²You will judge in my favour,
because you know what is right.

³You know my heart.
You have come to me at night;
you have examined me completely
and found no evil desire in me.
⁴I speak no evil as others do;
I have obeyed your command
and have not followed paths of violence.
⁵I have always walked in your way
and have never strayed from it.

⁶I pray to you, O God, because you answer me;
so turn to me and listen to my words.
⁷Reveal your wonderful love and save me;
at your side I am safe from my enemies.

⁸Protect me as you would your very eyes;
hide me in the shadow of your wings
⁹ from the attacks of the wicked.

Deadly enemies surround me;
¹⁰ they have no pity and speak proudly.
¹¹They are round me now, wherever I turn,
watching for a chance to pull me down.

**Protect me
as you would your very eyes;
hide me
in the shadow of your wings
from the attacks of the wicked.**

---

¹²They are like lions, waiting for me,
wanting to tear me to pieces.

¹³Come, LORD! Oppose my enemies and defeat
them!
Save me from the wicked by your sword;
¹⁴ save me from those who in this life have
all they want.
Punish them with the sufferings you have
stored up for them;

may there be enough for their children
and some left over for their children's
    children!

15But I will see you, because I have done no
    wrong;
    and when I awake, your presence will fill
    me with joy.

David's Song of Victory

18

How I love you, LORD!
    You are my defender.

2The LORD is my protector;
    he is my strong fortress.
My God is my protection,
    and with him I am safe.
He protects me like a shield;
    he defends me and keeps me safe.
3I call to the LORD,
    and he saves me from my enemies.
Praise the LORD!

4The danger of death was all round me;
    the waves of destruction rolled over me.
5The danger of death was round me,
    and the grave set its trap for me.
6In my trouble I called to the LORD;
    I called to my God for help.
In his temple he heard my voice;
    he listened to my cry for help.

7Then the earth trembled and shook;
    the foundations of the mountains rocked
    and quivered,
    because God was angry.
8Smoke poured out of his nostrils,
    a consuming flame and burning coals
    from his mouth.
9He tore the sky apart and came down
    with a dark cloud under his feet.
10He flew swiftly on a winged creature;
    he travelled on the wings of the wind.
11He covered himself with darkness;

thick clouds, full of water, surrounded
    him.
12Hailstones and flashes of fire
    came from the lightning before him
    and broke through the dark clouds.

13Then the LORD thundered from the sky;
    and the voice of the Most High was heard.
14He shot his arrows and scattered his
    enemies;
    with flashes of lightning he sent them
    running.
15The floor of the ocean was laid bare,
    and the foundations of the earth were
    uncovered,
when you rebuked your enemies, LORD,
    and roared at them in anger.

16The LORD reached down from above and
    took hold of me;
    he pulled me out of the deep waters.
17He rescued me from my powerful enemies
    and from all those who hate me—
    they were too strong for me.
18When I was in trouble, they attacked me,
    but the LORD protected me.
19He helped me out of danger;
    he saved me because he was pleased with
    me.

20The LORD rewards me because I do what is
    right;
    he blesses me because I am innocent.
21I have obeyed the law of the LORD;
    I have not turned away from my God.
22I have observed all his laws;
    I have not disobeyed his commands.
23He knows that I am faultless,
    that I have kept myself from doing wrong.
24And so he rewards me because I do what is
    right,
    because he knows that I am innocent.

25O LORD, you are faithful to those who are
    faithful to you;

'The LORD is my protector; he is my strong fortress.' (Psalm 18.2) ▷

completely good to those who are perfect.
²⁶You are pure to those who are pure,
but hostile to those who are wicked.
²⁷You save those who are humble,
but you humble those who are proud.

²⁸O LORD, you give me light;
you dispel my darkness.

O LORD, you give me light.

---

²⁹You give me strength to attack my enemies
and power to overcome their defences.

³⁰This God—how perfect are his deeds!
How dependable his words!
He is like a shield
for all who seek his protection.
³¹The LORD alone is God;
God alone is our defence.
³²He is the God who makes me strong,
who makes my pathway safe.
³³He makes me sure-footed as a deer;
he keeps me safe on the mountains.
³⁴He trains me for battle,
so that I can use the strongest bow.

³⁵O LORD, you protect me and save me;
your care has made me great,
and your power has kept me safe.
³⁶You have kept me from being captured,
and I have never fallen.
³⁷I pursue my enemies and catch them;
I do not stop until I destroy them.
³⁸I strike them down, and they cannot rise;
they lie defeated before me.
³⁹You give me strength for the battle
and victory over my enemies.
⁴⁰You make my enemies run from me;
I destroy those who hate me.
⁴¹They cry for help, but no one saves them;
they call to the LORD, but he does not
answer.
⁴²I crush them, so that they become like dust
which the wind blows away.
I trample on them like mud in the streets.

⁴³You saved me from a rebellious people
and made me ruler over the nations;

people I did not know have now become
my subjects.
⁴⁴Foreigners bow before me;
when they hear me, they obey.
⁴⁵They lose their courage
and come trembling from their fortresses.

⁴⁶The LORD lives! Praise my defender!
Proclaim the greatness of the God who
saves me.
⁴⁷He gives me victory over my enemies;
he subdues the nations under me
⁴⁸   and saves me from my foes.

O LORD, you give me victory over my enemies
and protect me from violent men.
⁴⁹And so I praise you among the nations;
I sing praises to you.

⁵⁰God gives great victories to his king;
he shows constant love to the one he has
chosen,
to David and his descendants for ever.

God's Glory in Creation

19
How clearly the sky reveals God's
glory!
How plainly it shows what he
has done!
²Each day announces it to the following day;
each night repeats it to the next.
³No speech or words are used,
no sound is heard;

**How clearly the sky
reveals God's glory!
How plainly it shows
what he has done!**

---

⁴yet their message goes out to all the world
and is heard to the ends of the earth.
God made a home in the sky for the sun;
⁵   it comes out in the morning like a happy
bridegroom,
like an athlete eager to run a race.
⁶It starts at one end of the sky
and goes across to the other.
Nothing can hide from its heat.

The Law of the LORD

⁷The law of the LORD is perfect;
    it gives new strength.
The commands of the LORD are trustworthy,
    giving wisdom to those who lack it.
⁸The laws of the LORD are right,
    and those who obey them are happy.
The commands of the LORD are just
    and give understanding to the mind.
⁹Reverence for the LORD is good;
    it will continue for ever.
The judgements of the LORD are just;
    they are always fair.
¹⁰They are more desirable than the finest gold;
    they are sweeter than the purest honey.
¹¹They give knowledge to me, your servant;
    I am rewarded for obeying them.

¹²No one can see his own errors;
    deliver me, LORD, from hidden faults!
¹³Keep me safe, also, from wilful sins;
    don't let them rule over me.
Then I shall be perfect
    and free from the evil of sin.

¹⁴May my words and my thoughts be
    acceptable to you,
O LORD, my refuge and my redeemer!

A Prayer for Victory

20 May the LORD answer you when
you are in trouble!
May the God of Jacob protect
you!
²May he send you help from his Temple
    and give you aid from Mount Zion.
³May he accept all your offerings
    and be pleased with all your sacrifices.

May the LORD answer you
when you are in trouble!

---

⁴May he give you what you desire
    and make all your plans succeed.
⁵Then we will shout for joy over your victory
    and celebrate your triumph by praising
    our God.
May the LORD answer all your requests.

⁶Now I know that the LORD gives victory to his
    chosen king;
he answers him from his holy heaven
    and by his power gives him great victories.

... we trust in the power
of the LORD our God.

---

⁷Some trust in their war-chariots
    and others in their horses,
    but we trust in the power of the LORD our
    God.
⁸Such people will stumble and fall,
    but we will rise and stand firm.

⁹Give victory to the king, O LORD;
    answer us when we call.

Praise for Victory

21 The king is glad, O LORD, because
you gave him strength;
he rejoices because you made
him victorious.
²You have given him his heart's desire;
    you have answered his request.

³You came to him with great blessings
    and set a crown of gold on his head.
⁴He asked for life, and you gave it,
    a long and lasting life.

⁵His glory is great because of your help;
    you have given him fame and majesty.
⁶Your blessings are with him for ever
    and your presence fills him with joy.

⁷The king trusts in the LORD Almighty;
    and because of the LORD's constant love
    he will always be secure.
⁸The king will capture all his enemies;
    he will capture everyone who hates him.
⁹He will destroy them like a blazing fire
    when he appears.

The LORD will devour them in his anger,
    and fire will consume them.
¹⁰None of their descendants will survive;
    the king will kill them all.

[11]They make their plans, and plot against him,
    but they will not succeed.
[12]He will shoot his arrows at them
    and make them turn and run.

[13]We praise you, LORD, for your great strength!
    We will sing and praise your power.

A Cry of Anguish and a Song of Praise

22
My God, my God, why have you
        abandoned me?
    I have cried desperately for help,
    but still it does not come.
[2]During the day I call to you, my God,
    but you do not answer;
I call at night,
    but get no rest.
[3]But you are enthroned as the Holy One,
    the one whom Israel praises.
[4]Our ancestors put their trust in you;
    they trusted you, and you saved them.
[5]They called to you and escaped from danger;
    they trusted you and were not
        disappointed.

[6]But I am no longer a man; I am a worm,
    despised and scorned by everyone!
[7]All who see me jeer at me;
    they stick out their tongues and shake
        their heads.
[8]'You relied on the LORD,' they say.
    'Why doesn't he save you?
If the LORD likes you,
    why doesn't he help you?'

[9]It was you who brought me safely through
      birth,
    and when I was a baby, you kept me safe.

**I have relied on you
since the day I was born,
and you have always been my God.**

---

[10]I have relied on you since the day I was born,
    and you have always been my God.
[11]Do not stay away from me!
    Trouble is near,
    and there is no one to help.

[12]Many enemies surround me like bulls;
    they are all round me,
    like fierce bulls from the land of Bashan.
[13]They open their mouths like lions,
    roaring and tearing at me.

[14]My strength is gone,
    gone like water spilt on the ground.
All my bones are out of joint;
    my heart is like melted wax.
[15]My throat is as dry as dust,
    and my tongue sticks to the roof of my
       mouth.
You have left me for dead in the dust.

[16]A gang of evil men is round me;
    like a pack of dogs they close in on me;
    they tear at my hands and feet.

**He does not neglect the poor
or ignore their suffering.**

---

[17]All my bones can be seen.
    My enemies look at me and stare.
[18]They gamble for my clothes
    and divide them among themselves.

[19]O LORD, don't stay away from me!
    Come quickly to my rescue!
[20]Save me from the sword;
    save my life from these dogs.
[21]Rescue me from these lions;
    I am helpless before these wild bulls.

[22]I will tell my people what you have done;
    I will praise you in their assembly:
[23]'Praise him, you servants of the LORD!
    Honour him, you descendants of Jacob!
    Worship him, you people of Israel!
[24]He does not neglect the poor or ignore their
      suffering;
    he does not turn away from them,
    but answers when they call for help.'

[25]In the full assembly I will praise you for what
      you have done;
    in the presence of those who worship you
    I will offer the sacrifices I promised.
[26]The poor will eat as much as they want;

those who come to the LORD will praise
  him.
May they prosper for ever!

²⁷All nations will remember the LORD.
  From every part of the world they will
    turn to him;
  all races will worship him.
²⁸The LORD is king,
  and he rules the nations.

**The LORD is king,
and he rules the nations.**

²⁹All proud men will bow down to him;
  all mortal men will bow down before him.
³⁰Future generations will serve him;
  men will speak of the Lord to the coming
    generation.
³¹People not yet born will be told:
  'The Lord saved his people.'

The LORD Our Shepherd

23 The LORD is my shepherd;
  I have everything I need.
²He lets me rest in fields of green
    grass
  and leads me to quiet pools of fresh water.
³He gives me new strength.
He guides me in the right paths,
  as he has promised.
⁴Even if I go through the deepest darkness,
  I will not be afraid, LORD,
  for you are with me.
Your shepherd's rod and staff protect
  me.

⁵You prepare a banquet for me,
  where all my enemies can see me;
you welcome me as an honoured guest
  and fill my cup to the brim.
⁶I know that your goodness and love will be
  with me all my life;
  and your house will be my home as long as
    I live.

'He lets me rest in fields of green grass and leads me to quiet pools of fresh water.' (Psalm 23.2)

The Great King

24

The world and all that is in it
belong to the LORD;
the earth and all who live on it
are his.
²He built it on the deep waters beneath the earth
and laid its foundations in the ocean depths.

³Who has the right to go up the LORD's hill?
Who may enter his holy Temple?
⁴Those who are pure in act and in thought,
who do not worship idols
or make false promises.
⁵The LORD will bless them and save them;
God will declare them innocent.
⁶Such are the people who come to God,
who come into the presence of the God of Jacob.

⁷Fling wide the gates,
open the ancient doors,
and the great king will come in.
⁸Who is this great king?
He is the LORD, strong and mighty,
the LORD, victorious in battle.

⁹Fling wide the gates,
open the ancient doors,
and the great king will come in.
¹⁰Who is this great king?
The triumphant LORD—he is the great king!

A Prayer for Guidance and Protection

25

To you, O LORD, I offer my prayer;
² in you, my God, I trust.
Save me from the shame of defeat;
don't let my enemies gloat over me!
³Defeat does not come to those who trust in you,
but to those who are quick to rebel against you.

⁴Teach me your ways, O LORD;
make them known to me.
⁵Teach me to live according to your truth,
for you are my God, who saves me.
I always trust in you.

⁶Remember, O LORD, your kindness and constant love
which you have shown from long ago.
⁷Forgive the sins and errors of my youth.
In your constant love and goodness,
remember me, LORD!

⁸Because the LORD is righteous and good,
he teaches sinners the path they should follow.
⁹He leads the humble in the right way
and teaches them his will.

He leads the humble in the right way...

---

¹⁰With faithfulness and love he leads
all who keep his covenant and obey his commands.

¹¹Keep your promise, LORD, and forgive my sins,
for they are many.
¹²Those who have reverence for the LORD
will learn from him the path they should follow.
¹³They will always be prosperous,
and their children will possess the land.
¹⁴The LORD is the friend of those who obey him
and he affirms his covenant with them.

¹⁵I look to the LORD for help at all times,
and he rescues me from danger.
¹⁶Turn to me, LORD, and be merciful to me,
because I am lonely and weak.
¹⁷Relieve me of my worries
and save me from all my troubles.
¹⁸Consider my distress and suffering
and forgive all my sins.

¹⁹See how many enemies I have;
see how much they hate me.
²⁰Protect me and save me;
keep me from defeat.
I come to you for safety.
²¹May my goodness and honesty preserve me,
because I trust in you.

²²From all their troubles, O God,
save your people Israel!

The Prayer of a Good Man

26

Declare me innocent, O LORD,
because I do what is right
and trust you completely.
²Examine me and test me, LORD;
judge my desires and thoughts.
³Your constant love is my guide;
your faithfulness always leads me.

⁴I do not keep company with worthless
people;
I have nothing to do with hypocrites.
⁵I hate the company of evil men
and avoid the wicked.

⁶LORD, I wash my hands to show that I am
innocent
and march in worship round your altar.
⁷I sing a hymn of thanksgiving
and tell of all your wonderful deeds.

⁸I love the house where you live, O LORD,
the place where your glory dwells.
⁹Do not destroy me with the sinners;
spare me from the fate of murderers—
¹⁰   men who do evil all the time
and are always ready to take bribes.

¹¹As for me, I do what is right;
be merciful to me and save me!

¹² I am safe from all dangers;
in the assembly of his people I praise the
LORD.

A Prayer of Praise

27

The LORD is my light and my
salvation;
I will fear no one.
The LORD protects me from all danger;
I will never be afraid.

**The LORD is my light
and my salvation;
I will fear no one.**

²When evil men attack me and try to kill me,
they stumble and fall.

³Even if a whole army surrounds me,
I will not be afraid;
even if enemies attack me,
I will still trust God.

⁴I have asked the LORD for one thing;
one thing only do I want:
to live in the LORD's house all my life,
to marvel there at his goodness,
and to ask for his guidance.
⁵In times of trouble he will shelter me;
he will keep me safe in his Temple
and make me secure on a high rock.
⁶So I will triumph over my enemies around
me.
With shouts of joy I will offer sacrifices in
his Temple;
I will sing, I will praise the LORD.

⁷Hear me, LORD, when I call to you!
Be merciful and answer me!

**My father and mother
may abandon me,
but the LORD will take care of me.**

⁸When you said, 'Come and worship me,'
I answered, 'I will come, LORD;
⁹   don't hide yourself from me!'

Don't be angry with me;
don't turn your servant away.
You have been my help;
don't leave me, don't abandon me,
O God, my saviour.
¹⁰My father and mother may abandon me,
but the LORD will take care of me.

¹¹Teach me, LORD, what you want me to do,
and lead me along a safe path,
because I have many enemies.
¹²Don't abandon me to my enemies,
who attack me with lies and threats.

¹³I know that I will live to see
the LORD's goodness in this present life.
¹⁴Trust in the LORD.
Have faith, do not despair.
Trust in the LORD.

A Prayer for Help

28 O LORD, my defender, I call to you.
Listen to my cry!
If you do not answer me,
I will be among those who go down to the
world of the dead.
²Hear me when I cry to you for help,
when I lift my hands towards your holy
Temple.
³Do not condemn me with the wicked,
with those who do evil—
men whose words are friendly,
but who have hatred in their hearts.

⁴Punish them for what they have done,
for the evil they have committed.

The LORD protects and defends me.

Punish them for all their deeds;
give them what they deserve!
⁵They take no notice of what the LORD has
done
or of what he has made;
so he will punish them
and destroy them for ever.

⁶Give praise to the LORD;
he has heard my cry for help.
⁷The LORD protects and defends me;
I trust in him.
He gives me help and makes me glad;
I praise him with joyful songs.

⁸The LORD protects his people;
he defends and saves his chosen king.
⁹Save your people, LORD,
and bless those who are yours.
Be their shepherd,
and take care of them for ever.

The Voice of the LORD in the Storm

29 Praise the LORD, you heavenly
beings;
praise his glory and power.
²Praise the LORD's glorious name;
bow down before the Holy One when he
appears.

³The voice of the LORD is heard on the seas;
the glorious God thunders,
and his voice echoes over the ocean.
⁴The voice of the LORD is heard
in all its might and majesty.

⁵The voice of the LORD breaks the cedars,
even the cedars of Lebanon.
⁶He makes the mountains of Lebanon jump
like calves
and makes Mount Hermon leap like a
young bull.

⁷The voice of the LORD makes the lightning
flash.
⁸His voice makes the desert shake;
he shakes the desert of Kadesh.
⁹The LORD's voice shakes the oaks
and strips the leaves from the trees
while everyone in his Temple shouts,
'Glory to God!'

¹⁰The LORD rules over the deep waters;
he rules as king for ever.
¹¹The LORD gives strength to his people
and blesses them with peace.

A Prayer of Thanksgiving

30 I praise you, LORD, because you
have saved me
and kept my enemies from
gloating over me.
²I cried to you for help, O LORD my God,
and you healed me;
³   you kept me from the grave.
I was on my way to the depths below,
but you restored my life.

⁴Sing praise to the LORD,
all his faithful people!
Remember what the Holy One has done,
and give him thanks!
⁵His anger lasts only a moment,
his goodness for a lifetime.
Tears may flow in the night,
but joy comes in the morning.

⁶I felt secure and said to myself,
'I will never be defeated.'
⁷You were good to me, LORD;

you protected me like a mountain fortress.
But then you hid yourself from me,
and I was afraid.

⁸I called to you, LORD;
I begged for your help:
⁹'What will you gain from my death?
What profit from my going to the grave?
Are dead people able to praise you?
Can they proclaim your unfailing
goodness?
¹⁰Hear me, LORD, and be merciful!
Help me, LORD!'

¹¹You have changed my sadness into a joyful
dance;
you have taken away my sorrow
and surrounded me with joy.
¹²So I will not be silent;
I will sing praise to you.
LORD, you are my God,
I will give you thanks for ever.

A Prayer of Trust in God

31
I come to you, LORD, for
protection;
never let me be defeated.
You are a righteous God;
save me, I pray!
²Hear me! Save me now!

Be my refuge to protect me;
my defence to save me.

³You are my refuge and defence;
guide me and lead me as you have
promised.
⁴Keep me safe from the trap that has been set
for me;
shelter me from danger.
⁵I place myself in your care.
You will save me, LORD;
you are a faithful God.

⁶You hate those who worship false gods,
but I trust in you.
⁷I will be glad and rejoice
because of your constant love.
You see my suffering;
you know my trouble.
⁸You have not let my enemies capture me;
you have given me freedom to go where I
wish.

⁹Be merciful to me, LORD,
for I am in trouble;
my eyes are tired from so much crying;
I am completely worn out.
¹⁰I am exhausted by sorrow,
and weeping has shortened my life.
I am weak from all my troubles;
even my bones are wasting away.

'You have taken away my sorrow and surrounded me with joy.' (Psalm 30.11)

¹¹All my enemies, and especially my
      neighbours,
   treat me with contempt;
 those who know me are afraid of me;
   when they see me in the street, they run
      away.
¹²Everyone has forgotten me, as though I
      were dead;
   I am like something thrown away.
¹³I hear many enemies whispering;
   terror is all round me.
 They are making plans against me,
   plotting to kill me.

¹⁴But my trust is in you, O LORD;
   you are my God.
¹⁵I am always in your care;
   save me from my enemies,
   from those who persecute me.

**Look on your servant
with kindness;
save me in your constant love.**

---

¹⁶Look on your servant with kindness;
   save me in your constant love.
¹⁷I call to you, LORD;
   don't let me be disgraced.
 May the wicked be disgraced;
   may they go silently down to the world of
      the dead.
¹⁸Silence those liars—
   all the proud and arrogant
   who speak with contempt about
      righteous men.

¹⁹How wonderful are the good things
   you keep for those who honour you!
 Everyone knows how good you are,
   how securely you protect those who trust
      you.
²⁰You hide them in the safety of your presence
   from the plots of men;
 in a safe shelter you hide them
   from the insults of their enemies.

²¹Praise the LORD!
 How wonderfully he showed his love for me
   when I was surrounded and attacked!

²²I was afraid and thought
   that he had driven me out of his presence.
 But he heard my cry,
   when I called to him for help.

²³Love the LORD, all his faithful people.
 The LORD protects the faithful,
   but punishes the proud as they deserve.
²⁴Be strong, be courageous,
   all you that hope in the LORD.

Confession and Forgiveness

32
Happy are those whose sins are
   forgiven,
   whose wrongs are pardoned.
²Happy is the man whom the LORD does not
   accuse of doing wrong
   and who is free from all deceit.

³When I did not confess my sins,
   I was worn out from crying all day long.
⁴Day and night you punished me, LORD;
   my strength was completely drained,
   as moisture is dried up by the summer
      heat.

⁵Then I confessed my sins to you;
   I did not conceal my wrongdoings.
 I decided to confess them to you,
   and you forgave all my sins.

⁶So all your loyal people should pray to you in
      times of need;
   when a great flood of trouble comes
      rushing in,
   it will not reach them.

**'I will teach you
the way you should go.'**

---

⁷You are my hiding place;
   you will save me from trouble.
 I sing aloud of your salvation,
   because you protect me.

⁸The LORD says, 'I will teach you the way you
      should go;
   I will instruct you and advise you.

9Don't be stupid like a horse or a mule,
  which must be controlled with a bit and
    bridle
  to make it submit.'

10The wicked will have to suffer,
  but those who trust in the LORD
  are protected by his constant love.
11You that are righteous, be glad and rejoice
  because of what the LORD has done.
  You that obey him, shout for joy!

A Song of Praise

33 All you that are righteous,
      shout for joy for what the LORD
        has done;
  praise him, all you that obey him.
2Give thanks to the LORD with harps,
  sing to him with stringed instruments.
3Sing a new song to him,
  play the harp with skill, and shout for joy!

4The words of the LORD are true
  and all his works are dependable.

**... shout for joy
for what the LORD has done.**

5The LORD loves what is righteous and just;
  his constant love fills the earth.

6The LORD created the heavens by his
    command,
  the sun, moon, and the stars by his spoken
    word.
7He gathered all the seas into one place;
  he shut up the ocean depths in
    storerooms.

8Worship the LORD, all the earth!
  Honour him, all peoples of the world!
9When he spoke, the world was created;
  at his command everything appeared.

10The LORD frustrates the purposes of the
    nations;
  he keeps them from carrying out their
    plans.

11But his plans endure for ever;
  his purposes last eternally.
12Happy is the nation whose God is the LORD;
  happy are the people he has chosen for his
    own!

13The LORD looks down from heaven
  and sees all mankind.
14From where he rules, he looks down
  on all who live on earth.
15He forms all their thoughts
  and knows everything they do.

16A king does not win because of his powerful
    army;
  a soldier does not triumph because of his
    strength.
17War-horses are useless for victory;
  their great strength cannot save.

18The LORD watches over those who obey him,
  those who trust in his constant love.
19He saves them from death;
  he keeps them alive in times of famine.

20We put our hope in the LORD;
  he is our protector and our help.
21We are glad because of him;
  we trust in his holy name.

22May your constant love be with us, LORD,
  as we put our hope in you.

In Praise of God's Goodness

34 I will always thank the LORD;
      I will never stop praising
        him.
2I will praise him for what he has done;
  may all who are oppressed listen and be
    glad!
3Proclaim with me the LORD's greatness;
  let us praise his name together!

4I prayed to the LORD, and he answered me;
  he freed me from all my fears.
5The oppressed look to him and are glad;
  they will never be disappointed.
6The helpless call to him, and he answers;
  he saves them from all their troubles.
7His angel guards those who honour the LORD

and rescues them from danger.

8Find out for yourself how good the LORD is.
　Happy are those who find safety with him.
9Honour the LORD, all his people;
　those who obey him have all they need.
10Even lions go hungry for lack of food,
　but those who obey the LORD lack nothing
　　good.

11Come, my young friends, and listen to me,
　and I will teach you to honour the LORD.
12Would you like to enjoy life?
　Do you want long life and happiness?
13Then hold back from speaking evil
　and from telling lies.
14Turn away from evil and do good;
　strive for peace with all your heart.

15The LORD watches over the righteous
　and listens to their cries;
16but he opposes those who do evil,
　so that when they die, they are soon
　　forgotten.
17The righteous call to the LORD, and he listens;
　he rescues them from all their troubles.
18The LORD is near to those who are
　　discouraged;
　he saves those who have lost all hope.

19The good man suffers many troubles,
　but the LORD saves him from them all;
20the LORD preserves him completely;
　not one of his bones is broken.
21Evil will kill the wicked;
　those who hate the righteous will be
　　punished.

22The LORD will save his people;
　those who go to him for protection will be
　　spared.

A Prayer for Help

35 Oppose those who oppose me,
　　LORD,
　　and fight those who fight
　　　against me!
2Take your shield and armour
　and come to my rescue.
3Lift up your spear and your axe
　against those who pursue me.
Promise that you will save me.

4May those who try to kill me
　be defeated and disgraced!
May those who plot against me
　be turned back and confused!
5May they be like straw blown by the wind
　as the angel of the LORD pursues them!
6May their path be dark and slippery
　while the angel of the LORD strikes them
　　down!

7Without any reason they laid a trap for me
　and dug a deep hole to catch me.
8But destruction will catch them before they
　　know it;
　they will be caught in their own trap
　and fall to their destruction!

9Then I will be glad because of the LORD;
　I will be happy because he saved me.

The LORD is near
to those who are discouraged.

10With all my heart I will say to the LORD,
　'There is no one like you.
　You will protect the weak from the
　　strong,
　the poor from the oppressor.'

11Evil men testify against me
　and accuse me of crimes I know nothing
　　about.
12They pay me back evil for good,
　and I sink in despair.
13But when they were sick, I dressed in
　　mourning;
　I deprived myself of food;
　I prayed with my head bowed low,
14　as I would pray for a friend or a brother.
　I went about bent over in mourning,
　as one who mourns for his mother.

15But when I was in trouble, they were all glad
　and gathered round to mock me;
　strangers beat me
　and kept striking me.

'Come, my young friends, and listen to me.' (Psalm 34.11)

¹⁶Like men who would mock a cripple,
    they glared at me with hate.

¹⁷How much longer, Lord, will you just look
    on?
    Rescue me from their attacks;
    save my life from these lions!
¹⁸Then I will thank you in the assembly of your
    people;
    I will praise you before them all.

¹⁹Don't let my enemies, those liars,
    gloat over my defeat.

**... I will proclaim your righteousness,
and I will praise you
all day long.**

Don't let those who hate me for no reason
    smirk with delight over my sorrow.

²⁰They do not speak in a friendly way;
    instead they invent all kinds of lies about
    peace-loving people.

²¹They accuse me, shouting,
    'We saw what you did!'
²²But you, O LORD, have seen this.
    So don't be silent, Lord;
    don't keep yourself far away!
²³Rouse yourself, O Lord, and defend me;
    rise up, my God, and plead my cause.
²⁴You are righteous, O LORD, so declare me
    innocent;
    don't let my enemies gloat over me.
²⁵Don't let them say to themselves,
    'We are rid of him!
    That's just what we wanted!'

²⁶May those who gloat over my suffering
    be completely defeated and confused;
    may those who claim to be better than I am
    be covered with shame and disgrace.

²⁷May those who want to see me acquitted
    shout for joy and say again and again,
    'How great is the LORD!
    He is pleased with the success of his
    servant.'
²⁸Then I will proclaim your righteousness,
    and I will praise you all day long.

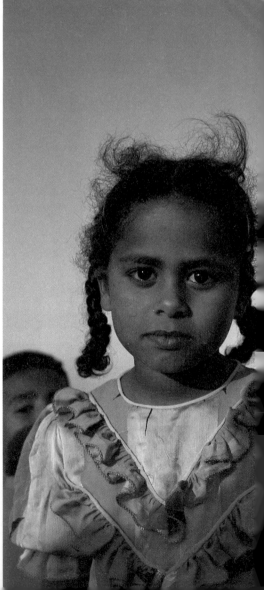

*Your praise
reaches up to the heavens;
it is sung
by children and babies.*

Psalm 8.1–2

The Wickedness of Man

36

Sin speaks to the wicked man
deep in his heart;
he rejects God and has no
reverence for him.
²Because he thinks so highly of himself,
he thinks that God will not discover his sin
and condemn it.
³His speech is wicked and full of lies;
he no longer does what is wise and good.
⁴He makes evil plans as he lies in bed;
nothing he does is good,
and he never rejects anything evil.

The Goodness of God

⁵LORD, your constant love reaches the
heavens;
your faithfulness extends to the skies.
⁶Your righteousness is towering like the
mountains;
your justice is like the depths of the sea.
Men and animals are in your care.

⁷How precious, O God, is your constant love!
We find protection under the shadow of
your wings.
⁸We feast on the abundant food you provide;
you let us drink from the river of your
goodness.
⁹You are the source of all life,
and because of your light we see the light.

¹⁰Continue to love those who know you
and to do good to those who are
righteous.
¹¹Do not let proud men attack me
or wicked men make me run away.

¹²See where evil men have fallen.
There they lie, unable to rise.

The Destiny of the Wicked and of the Good

37

Don't be worried on account of
the wicked;
don't be jealous of those who
do wrong.
²They will soon disappear like grass that dries
up;
they will die like plants that wither.

³Trust in the LORD and do good;
live in the land and be safe.
⁴Seek your happiness in the LORD,
and he will give you your heart's desire.

⁵Give yourself to the LORD;
trust in him, and he will help you;
⁶he will make your righteousness shine like
the noonday sun.

⁷Be patient and wait for the LORD to act;
don't be worried about those who prosper
or those who succeed in their evil plans.

⁸Don't give in to worry or anger;
it only leads to trouble.
⁹Those who trust in the LORD will possess the
land,
but the wicked will be driven out.

¹⁰Soon the wicked will disappear;
you may look for them, but you won't find
them;
¹¹the humble will possess the land
and enjoy prosperity and peace.

¹²The wicked man plots against the good man
and glares at him with hate.

**Don't give in to worry or anger;
it only leads to trouble.**

---

¹³But the Lord laughs at wicked men,
because he knows they will soon be
destroyed.

¹⁴The wicked draw their swords and bend
their bows
to kill the poor and needy,
to slaughter those who do what is right;
¹⁵but they will be killed by their own swords,
and their bows will be smashed.

¹⁶The little that a good man owns
is worth more than the wealth of all the
wicked,
¹⁷because the LORD will take away the strength
of the wicked,
but protect those who are good.

[18]The LORD takes care of those who obey him,
    and the land will be theirs for ever.
[19]They will not suffer when times are bad;
    they will have enough in time of famine.

**Turn away from evil
and do good ...**

---

[20]But the wicked will die;
    the enemies of the LORD will vanish like
      wild flowers;
    they will disappear like smoke.

[21]The wicked man borrows and never pays
      back,
    but the good man is generous with his
      gifts.
[22]Those who are blessed by the LORD will
      possess the land,
    but those who are cursed by him will be
      driven out.

[23]The LORD guides a man in the way he should
      go
    and protects those who please him.
[24]If they fall, they will not stay down,
    because the LORD will help them up.

[25]I am an old man now; I have lived a long time,
    but I have never seen a good man
      abandoned by the LORD
    or his children begging for food.
[26]At all times he gives freely and lends to
      others,
    and his children are a blessing.

[27]Turn away from evil and do good,
    and your descendants will always live in
      the land;
[28]for the LORD loves what is right
    and does not abandon his faithful people.
  He protects them for ever,
    but the descendants of the wicked will be
      driven out.
[29]The righteous will possess the land
    and live in it for ever.

[30]A good man's words are wise,
    and he is always fair.

[31]He keeps the law of his God in his heart
    and never departs from it.

[32]A wicked man watches a good man
    and tries to kill him;
[33]but the LORD will not abandon him to his
  ·   enemy's power
    or let him be condemned when he is on
      trial.

[34]Put your hope in the LORD and obey his
      commands;
    he will honour you by giving you the land,
    and you will see the wicked driven out.

[35]I once knew a wicked man who was a tyrant;
    he towered over everyone like a cedar of
      Lebanon;
[36]but later I passed by, and he wasn't there;
    I looked for him, but couldn't find him.

[37]Notice the good man, observe the righteous
      man;
    a peaceful man has descendants,
[38]but sinners are completely destroyed,
    and their descendants are wiped out.

[39]The LORD saves righteous men
    and protects them in times of trouble.
[40]He helps them and rescues them;
    he saves them from the wicked,
    because they go to him for protection.

The Prayer of a Suffering Man

38 O LORD, don't punish me in your
      anger!
[2]You have wounded me with your
      arrows;
    you have struck me down.

[3]Because of your anger, I am in great pain;
    my whole body is diseased because of my
      sins.   ·
[4]I am drowning in the flood of my sins;
    they are a burden too heavy to bear.

[5]Because I have been foolish,
    my sores stink and rot.
[6]I am bowed down, I am crushed;
    I mourn all day long.

⁷I am burning with fever
      and I am near to death.
⁸I am worn out and utterly crushed;
      my heart is troubled, and I groan with
        pain.

⁹O Lord, you know what I long for;
      you hear all my groans.
¹⁰My heart is pounding, my strength is gone,
      and my eyes have lost their brightness.
¹¹My friends and neighbours will not come
        near me,
      because of my sores;
      even my family keeps away from me.
¹²Those who want to kill me lay traps for me,
      and those who want to hurt me threaten
        to ruin me;
      they never stop plotting against me.

¹³I am like a deaf man and cannot hear,
      like a dumb man and cannot speak.
¹⁴I am like a man who does not answer,
      because he cannot hear.

¹⁵But I trust in you, O LORD;
      and you, O Lord my God, will answer me.
¹⁶Don't let my enemies gloat over my distress;
      don't let them boast about my downfall!
¹⁷I am about to fall
      and am in constant pain.

¹⁸I confess my sins;
      they fill me with anxiety.
¹⁹My enemies are healthy and strong;
      there are many who hate me for no
        reason.
²⁰Those who pay back evil for good
      are against me because I try to do right.

²¹Do not abandon me, O LORD;
      do not stay away, my God!
²²Help me now, O Lord my saviour!

The Confession of a Suffering Man

39

I said, 'I will be careful what I do
      and will not let my tongue
        make me sin;
I will not say anything
      while evil men are near.'
²I kept quiet, not saying a word,

not even about anything good!
But my suffering only grew worse,
³   and I was overcome with anxiety.

Save me from all my sins ...

The more I thought, the more troubled I
        became;
      I could not keep from asking:
⁴'LORD, how long will I live?
      When will I die?
      Tell me how soon my life will end.'

⁵How short you have made my life!
      In your sight my lifetime seems nothing.
Indeed every living man is no more than a
        puff of wind,
⁶   no more than a shadow.
All he does is for nothing;
      he gathers wealth, but doesn't know who
        will get it.

⁷What, then, can I hope for, Lord?
      I put my hope in you.
⁸Save me from all my sins,
      and don't let fools laugh at me.
⁹I will keep quiet, I will not say a word,
      for you are the one who made me suffer
        like this.

Hear my prayer, LORD,
and listen to my cry.

¹⁰Don't punish me any more!
      I am about to die from your blows.
¹¹You punish a man's sins by your rebukes,
      and like a moth you destroy what he loves.
Indeed a man is no more than a puff of wind!

¹²Hear my prayer, LORD,
      and listen to my cry;
      come to my aid when I weep.
Like all my ancestors
      I am only your guest for a little while.
¹³Leave me alone so that I may have some
        happiness
      before I go away and am no more.

'I put my hope in you.' (Psalm 39.7)

A Song of Praise

40

I waited patiently for the LORD's
    help;
    then he listened to me and
    heard my cry.
²He pulled me out of a dangerous pit,
    out of the deadly quicksand.
He set me safely on a rock
    and made me secure.
³He taught me to sing a new song,
    a song of praise to our God.

**'How I love
to do your will, my God!
I keep your teaching
in my heart.'**

Many who see this will take warning
    and will put their trust in the LORD.

⁴Happy are those who trust the LORD,
    who do not turn to idols
    or join those who worship false gods.
⁵You have done many things for us, O LORD
    our God;
    there is no one like you!
    You have made many wonderful plans for
    us.
I could never speak of them all—
    their number is so great!

⁶You do not want sacrifices and offerings;
    you do not ask for animals burnt whole on
    the altar
    or for sacrifices to take away sins.
Instead, you have given me ears to hear you,
⁷   and so I answered, 'Here I am;
    your instructions for me are in the book
    of the Law.
⁸How I love to do your will, my God!
    I keep your teaching in my heart.'

⁹In the assembly of all your people, LORD,
    I told the good news that you save us.
    You know that I will never stop telling it.
¹⁰I have not kept the news of salvation to
    myself;
    I have always spoken of your faithfulness
    and help.

In the assembly of all your people I have not
    been silent
    about your loyalty and constant love.

¹¹LORD, I know you will never stop being
    merciful to me.
    Your love and loyalty will always keep me
    safe.

A Prayer for Help

¹²I am surrounded by many troubles—
    too many to count!
My sins have caught up with me,
    and I can no longer see;
they are more than the hairs of my head,
    and I have lost my courage.
¹³Save me, LORD! Help me now!
¹⁴May those who try to kill me
    be completely defeated and confused.
May those who are happy because of my
    troubles
    be turned back and disgraced.
¹⁵May those who jeer at me
    be dismayed by their defeat.

¹⁶May all who come to you
    be glad and joyful.
May all who are thankful for your salvation
    always say, 'How great is the LORD!'

¹⁷I am weak and poor, O Lord,
    but you have not forgotten me.
You are my saviour and my God—
    hurry to my aid!

The Prayer of a Sick Man

41

Happy are those who are
    concerned for the poor;
    the LORD will help them when
    they are in trouble.
²The LORD will protect them and preserve
    their lives;
    he will make them happy in the land;
    he will not abandon them to the power of
    their enemies.
³The LORD will help them when they are sick
    and will restore them to health.

⁴I said, 'I have sinned against you, LORD;
    be merciful to me and heal me.'

⁵My enemies say cruel things about me.
    They want me to die and be forgotten.
⁶Those who come to see me are not sincere;
    they gather bad news about me
and then go out and tell it everywhere.
⁷All who hate me whisper to each other about
        me,
    they imagine the worst about me.
⁸They say, 'He is fatally ill;
    he will never leave his bed again.'
⁹Even my best friend, the one I trusted most,
    the one who shared my food,
    has turned against me.

¹⁰Be merciful to me, LORD, and restore my
        health,
    and I will pay my enemies back.
¹¹They will not triumph over me,
    and I will know that you are pleased with
        me.
¹²You will help me, because I do what is right;
    you will keep me in your presence for
        ever.

'He pulled me out of a dangerous pit ...' (Psalm 40.2)

¹³Praise the LORD, the God of Israel!
    Praise him now and for ever!

Amen! Amen!

BOOK TWO
(Psalms 42–72)

The Prayer of a Man in Exile

42 As a deer longs for a stream of
cool water,
so I long for you, O God.
²I thirst for you, the living God;
when can I go and worship in your
presence?
³Day and night I cry,
and tears are my only food;
all the time my enemies ask me,
'Where is your God?'

⁴My heart breaks when I remember the past,
when I went with the crowds to the house
of God
and led them as they walked along,
a happy crowd, singing and shouting
praise to God.

**As a deer longs for
a stream of cool water,
so I long for you, O God.**

---

⁵Why am I so sad?
Why am I so troubled?
I will put my hope in God,
and once again I will praise him,
my saviour and my God.

⁶⁻⁷Here in exile my heart is breaking,
and so I turn my thoughts to him.
He has sent waves of sorrow over my soul;
chaos roars at me like a flood,
like waterfalls thundering down to the
Jordan
from Mount Hermon and Mount Mizar.
⁸May the LORD show his constant love during
the day,
so that I may have a song at night,
a prayer to the God of my life.

⁹To God, my defender, I say,
'Why have you forgotten me?
Why must I go on suffering
from the cruelty of my enemies?'

¹⁰I am crushed by their insults,
as they keep on asking me,
'Where is your God?'

¹¹Why am I so sad?
Why am I so troubled?
I will put my hope in God,
and once again I will praise him,
my saviour and my God.

The Prayer of a Man in Exile
(Continuation of Psalm 42)

43 O God, declare me innocent,
and defend my cause against
the ungodly;
deliver me from lying and evil men!
²You are my protector;
why have you abandoned me?
Why must I go on suffering
from the cruelty of my enemies?

³Send your light and your truth;
may they lead me
and bring me back to Zion, your sacred
hill,
and to your Temple, where you live.
⁴Then I will go to your altar, O God;
you are the source of my happiness.

**Send your light
and your truth.**

I will play my harp and sing praise to you,
O God, my God.

⁵Why am I so sad?
Why am I so troubled?
I will put my hope in God,
and once again I will praise him,
my saviour and my God.

A Prayer for Protection

44 With our own ears we have heard
it, O God—
our ancestors have told us
about it,
about the great things you did in their time,

in the days of long ago:
²how you yourself drove out the heathen
and established your people in their land;
how you punished the other nations
and caused your own to prosper.
³Your people did not conquer the land with
their swords;
they did not win it by their own power;
it was by your power and your strength,
by the assurance of your presence,
which showed that you loved them.

⁴You are my king and my God;
you give victory to your people,

¹²You sold your own people for a small
price
as though they had little value.

¹³Our neighbours see what you did to us,
and they mock us and laugh at us.
¹⁴You have made us an object of contempt
among the nations;
they shake their heads at us in scorn.
¹⁵I am always in disgrace;
I am covered with shame
¹⁶ from hearing the sneers and insults
of my enemies and those who hate
me.

'As a deer longs for a stream of cool water, so I long for you, O God.' (Psalm 42.1)

⁵ and by your power we defeat our
enemies.
⁶I do not trust in my bow
or in my sword to save me;
⁷but you have saved us from our enemies
and defeated those who hate us.
⁸We will always praise you
and give thanks to you for ever.

⁹But now you have rejected us and let us be
defeated;
you no longer march out with our armies.
¹⁰You made us run from our enemies,
and they took for themselves what was
ours.
¹¹You allowed us to be slaughtered like sheep;
you scattered us in foreign countries.

¹⁷All this has happened to us,
even though we have not forgotten you
or broken the covenant you made with us.
¹⁸We have not been disloyal to you;
we have not disobeyed your commands.
¹⁹Yet you left us helpless among wild animals;
you abandoned us in deepest darkness.

²⁰If we had stopped worshipping our God
and prayed to a foreign god,
²¹you would surely have discovered it,
because you know our secret thoughts.
²²But it is on your account that we are being
killed all the time,
that we are treated like sheep to be
slaughtered.

²³Wake up, Lord! Why are you asleep?
  Rouse yourself! Don't reject us for ever!
²⁴Why are you hiding from us?
  Don't forget our suffering and trouble!

Come to our aid!

---

²⁵We fall crushed to the ground;
  we lie defeated in the dust.
²⁶Come to our aid!
  Because of your constant love save us!

A Royal Wedding Song

45 Beautiful words fill my mind,
  as I compose this song for the
  king.
Like the pen of a good writer
  my tongue is ready with a poem.

²You are the most handsome of men;
  you are an eloquent speaker.
  God has always blessed you.
³Buckle on your sword, mighty king;
  you are glorious and majestic.

⁴Ride on in majesty to victory
  for the defence of truth and justice!
  Your strength will win you great victories!
⁵Your arrows are sharp,
  they pierce the hearts of your enemies;
  nations fall down at your feet.

⁶The kingdom that God has given you
  will last for ever and ever.
You rule over your people with justice;
⁷ you love what is right and hate what is evil.
That is why God, your God, has chosen you
  and has poured out more happiness on
    you
  than on any other king.
⁸The perfume of myrrh and aloes is on your
    clothes;
  musicians entertain you in palaces
    decorated with ivory.
⁹Among the ladies of your court are
    daughters of kings,
  and on the right of your throne stands the
    queen,

wearing ornaments of finest gold.

¹⁰Bride of the king, listen to what I say—
  forget your people and your relatives.
¹¹Your beauty will make the king desire you;
  he is your master, so you must obey him.
¹²The people of Tyre will bring you gifts;
  rich people will try to win your favour.

¹³The princess is in the palace—how beautiful
    she is!
  Her gown is made of gold thread.
¹⁴In her colourful gown she is led to the king,
  followed by her bridesmaids,
  and they also are brought to him.
¹⁵With joy and gladness they come
  and enter the king's palace.

¹⁶You, my king, will have many sons
  to succeed your ancestors as kings,
  and you will make them rulers over the
    whole earth.
¹⁷My song will keep your fame alive for ever,
  and everyone will praise you for all time
    to come.

God Is with Us

46 God is our shelter and strength,
  always ready to help in times
  of trouble.
²So we will not be afraid, even if the earth is
    shaken
  and mountains fall into the ocean depths;
³even if the seas roar and rage,
  and the hills are shaken by the violence.

God is our shelter and strength, always ready to help in times of trouble.

---

⁴There is a river that brings joy to the city of
    God,
  to the sacred house of the Most High.
⁵God is in that city, and it will never be
    destroyed;
  at early dawn he will come to its aid.
⁶Nations are terrified, kingdoms are shaken;
  God thunders, and the earth dissolves.

[7]The LORD Almighty is with us;
the God of Jacob is our refuge.

[8]Come and see what the LORD has done.
See what amazing things he has done on
earth.
[9]He stops wars all over the world;
he breaks bows, destroys spears,
and sets shields on fire.
[10]'Stop fighting,' he says, 'and know that I am
God,
supreme among the nations,
supreme over the world.'

[11]The LORD almighty is with us;
the God of Jacob is our refuge.

The Supreme Ruler

47 Clap your hands for joy, all
peoples!
Praise God with loud songs!
[2]The LORD, the Most High, is to be feared;
he is a great king, ruling over all the world.
[3]He gave us victory over the peoples;
he made us rule over the nations.
[4]He chose for us the land where we live,

**God is king over all the world;
praise him with songs!**

---

the proud possession of his people, whom
he loves.

[5]God goes up to his throne.
There are shouts of joy and the blast of
trumpets,
as the LORD goes up.
[6]Sing praise to God;
sing praise to our king!
[7]God is king over all the world;
praise him with songs!

[8]God sits on his sacred throne;
he rules over the nations.
[9]The rulers of the nations assemble
with the people of the God of Abraham.
More powerful than all armies is he;
he rules supreme.

Zion, the City of God

48 The LORD is great and is to be
highly praised
in the city of our God, on his
sacred hill.
[2]Zion, the mountain of God, is high and
beautiful;
the city of the great king brings joy to all
the world.
[3]God has shown that there is safety with him
inside the fortresses of the city.

[4]The kings gathered together
and came to attack Mount Zion.
[5]But when they saw it, they were amazed;
they were afraid and ran away.
[6]There they were seized with fear and
anguish,
like a woman about to bear a child,
[7]   like ships tossing in a furious storm.

[8]We have heard what God has done,
and now we have seen it
in the city of our God, the LORD Almighty;
he will keep the city safe for ever.

[9]Inside your Temple, O God,
we think of your constant love.
[10]You are praised by people everywhere,
and your fame extends over all the earth.
You rule with justice;
[11]   let the people of Zion be glad!
You give right judgements;
let there be joy in the cities of Judah!

[12]People of God, walk round Zion and count
the towers;
[13]   take notice of the walls and examine the
fortresses,
so that you may tell the next generation:
[14]   'This God is our God for ever and ever;
he will lead us for all time to come.'

The Foolishness of Trusting in Riches

49 Hear this, everyone!
Listen, all people everywhere,
[2]   great and small alike,
rich and poor together.
[3]My thoughts will be clear;
I will speak words of wisdom.

⁴I will turn my attention to proverbs
  and explain their meaning as I play the
    harp.

⁵I am not afraid in times of danger
  when I am surrounded by enemies,
⁶by evil men who trust in their riches
  and boast of their great wealth.
⁷A person can never redeem himself;
  he cannot pay God the price for his life,
⁸   because the payment for a human life is
    too great.
What he could pay would never be enough
⁹   to keep him from the grave,
  to let him live for ever.

¹⁰Anyone can see that even wise men die,
  as well as foolish and stupid men.
  They all leave their riches to their
    descendants.
¹¹Their graves are their homes for ever;
  there they stay for all time,
  though they once had lands of their own.

A man's greatness
cannot save him from death.

---

¹²A man's greatness cannot save him from
    death;
  he will still die like the animals.

¹³See what happens to those who trust in
    themselves,
  the fate of those who are satisfied with
    their wealth—
¹⁴they are doomed to die like sheep,
  and Death will be their shepherd.
The righteous will triumph over them,
  as their bodies quickly decay
  in the world of the dead far from their
    homes.
¹⁵But God will rescue me;
  he will save me from the power of death.

¹⁶Don't be upset when a man becomes rich,
  when his wealth grows even greater;
¹⁷he cannot take it with him when he dies;
  his wealth will not go with him to the
    grave.

¹⁸Even if a man is satisfied with this life
  and is praised because he is successful,
¹⁹he will join his ancestors in death,
  where the darkness lasts for ever.
²⁰A man's greatness cannot save him from
    death;
  he will still die like the animals.

True Worship

50 The Almighty God, the LORD,
    speaks;
  he calls to the whole earth
    from east to west.
²God shines from Zion,
  the city perfect in its beauty.

³Our God is coming, but not in silence;
  a raging fire is in front of him,
  a furious storm is round him.
⁴He calls heaven and earth as witnesses
  to see him judge his people.
⁵He says, 'Gather my faithful people to me,
  those who made a covenant with me by
    offering a sacrifice.'
⁶The heavens proclaim that God is righteous,
  that he himself is judge.

⁷'Listen, my people, and I will speak;
  I will testify against you, Israel.
  I am God, your God.
⁸I do not reprimand you because of your
    sacrifices
  and the burnt-offerings you always bring
    me.
⁹And yet I do not need bulls from your farms
  or goats from your flocks;
¹⁰all the animals in the forest are mine
  and the cattle on thousands of hills.

'... the world and
everything in it is mine.'

---

¹¹All the wild birds are mine
  and all living things in the fields.

¹²'If I were hungry, I would not ask you for
    food,
  for the world and everything in it is mine.

'Remove my sin, and I will be clean; wash me, and I will be whiter than snow.' (Psalm 51.7)

¹³Do I eat the flesh of bulls
 or drink the blood of goats?
¹⁴Let the giving of thanks be your sacrifice to
  God,
 and give the Almighty all that you
  promised.
¹⁵Call to me when trouble comes;
 I will save you,
 and you will praise me.'

¹⁶But God says to the wicked,
 'Why should you recite my commandments?
 Why should you talk about my covenant?
¹⁷You refuse to let me correct you;
 you reject my commands.

'Call to me when trouble comes.'

---

¹⁸You become the friend of every thief you see
 and you associate with adulterers.

¹⁹'You are always ready to speak evil;
 you never hesitate to tell lies.
²⁰You are ready to accuse your own brothers
 and to find fault with them.
²¹You have done all this, and I have said
  nothing,
 so you thought that I was like you.
 But now I reprimand you

and make the matter plain to you.

²²'Listen to this, you that ignore me,
 or I will destroy you,
 and there will be no one to save you.
²³Giving thanks is the sacrifice that honours
  me,
 and I will surely save all who obey me.'

A Prayer for Forgiveness

51
 Be merciful to me, O God,
   because of your constant love.
   Because of your great mercy
 wipe away my sins!
²Wash away all my evil
 and make me clean from my sin!

³I recognize my faults;
 I am always conscious of my sins.
⁴I have sinned against you—only against
  you—
 and done what you consider evil.
 So you are right in judging me;
 you are justified in condemning me.
⁵I have been evil from the day I was born;
 from the time I was conceived, I have been
  sinful.

⁶Sincerity and truth are what you require;
 fill my mind with your wisdom.
⁷Remove my sin, and I will be clean;

wash me, and I will be whiter than snow.
8Let me hear the sounds of joy and gladness;
   and though you have crushed me and
      broken me,
   I will be happy once again.
9Close your eyes to my sins
   and wipe out all my evil.

10Create a pure heart in me, O God,
   and put a new and loyal spirit in me.

Create a pure heart in me ...

11Do not banish me from your presence;
   do not take your holy spirit away from me.
12Give me again the joy that comes from your
      salvation,
   and make me willing to obey you.
13Then I will teach sinners your commands,
   and they will turn back to you.

14Spare my life, O God, and save me,
   and I will gladly proclaim your
      righteousness.
15Help me to speak, Lord,
   and I will praise you.

16You do not want sacrifices,
   or I would offer them;
   you are not pleased with burnt-offerings.
17My sacrifice is a humble spirit, O God;
   you will not reject a humble and repentant
      heart.

18O God, be kind to Zion and help her;
   rebuild the walls of Jerusalem.
19Then you will be pleased with proper
      sacrifices
   and with our burnt-offerings;
   and bulls will be sacrificed on your altar.

God's Judgement and Grace
52 Why do you boast, great man,
         of your evil?
      God's faithfulness is eternal.
2You make plans to ruin others;
   your tongue is like a sharp razor.
   You are always inventing lies.

3You love evil more than good
   and falsehood more than truth.
4You love to hurt people with your words,
   you liar!

5So God will ruin you for ever;
   he will take hold of you and snatch you
      from your home;
   he will remove you from the world of the
      living.
6Righteous people will see this and be afraid;
   then they will laugh at you and say,
7'Look, here is a man who did not depend on
      God for safety,
   but trusted instead in his great wealth
   and looked for security in being wicked.'

8But I am like an olive-tree growing in the
      house of God;
   I trust in his constant love for ever and
      ever.

God's faithfulness is eternal.

9I will always thank you, God, for what you
      have done;
   in the presence of your people
   I will proclaim that you are good.

The Wickedness of Men
53 Fools say to themselves,
         'There is no God.'
      They are all corrupt,
   and they have done terrible things;
   there is no one who does what is right.

2God looks down from heaven at mankind
   to see if there are any who are wise,
   any who worship him.
3But they have all turned away;
   they are all equally bad.
Not one of them does what is right,
   not a single one.

4'Don't they know?' God asks.
   'Are these evildoers ignorant?
   They live by robbing my people,
   and they never pray to me.'

⁵But then they will be terrified,
  as they have never been before,
  for God will scatter the bones of the
    enemies of his people.
God has rejected them,
  and so Israel will totally defeat them.

⁶How I pray that victory
  will come to Israel from Zion.
How happy the people of Israel will be
  when God makes them prosperous again!

A Prayer for Protection from Enemies

54 Save me by your power, O God;
      set me free by your might!
²Hear my prayer, O God;
  listen to my words!
³Proud men are coming to attack me;
  cruel men are trying to kill me—
  men who do not care about God.

⁴But God is my helper.
  The Lord is my defender.
⁵May God use their own evil to punish my
    enemies.
  He will destroy them because he is
    faithful.

⁶I will gladly offer you a sacrifice, O LORD;
  I will give you thanks
  because you are good.
⁷You have rescued me from all my troubles,
  and I have seen my enemies defeated.

The Prayer of a Man Betrayed by a Friend

55 Hear my prayer, O God;
      don't turn away from my plea!
²Listen to me, and answer me;
  I am worn out by my worries.
³I am terrified by the threats of my enemies,
  crushed by the oppression of the wicked.
They bring trouble on me;
  they are angry with me and hate me.

⁴I am terrified,
  and the terrors of death crush me.
⁵I am gripped by fear and trembling;
  I am overcome with horror.
⁶I wish I had wings, like a dove.

I would fly away and find rest.
⁷I would fly far away
  and live in the wilderness.
⁸I would quickly find myself a shelter
  from the raging wind and the storm.
⁹Confuse the speech of my enemies, O Lord!

I see violence and riots in the city,
¹⁰ surrounding it day and night,
  filling it with crime and trouble.
¹¹There is destruction everywhere;
  the streets are full of oppression and
    fraud.

¹²If it were an enemy that mocked me,
  I could endure it;
if it were an opponent boasting over me,
  I could hide myself from him.
¹³But it is you, my companion,
  my colleague and close friend.
¹⁴We had intimate talks with each other
  and worshipped together in the Temple.
¹⁵May my enemies die before their time;
  may they go down alive into the world of
    the dead!
Evil is in their homes and in their hearts.

'I am worn out by my worries.' (Psalm 55.2)

¹⁶But I call to the LORD God for help,
and he will save me.
¹⁷Morning, noon, and night
my complaints and groans go up to him,
and he will hear my voice.
¹⁸He will bring me safely back
from the battles that I fight
against so many enemies.
¹⁹God, who has ruled from eternity,
will hear me and defeat them;
for they refuse to change,
and they do not fear him.

²⁰My former companion attacked his friends;
he broke his promises.
²¹His words were smoother than cream,
but there was hatred in his heart;
his words were as soothing as oil,
but they cut like sharp swords.

²²Leave your troubles with the LORD,
and he will defend you;
he never lets honest men be defeated.

²³But you, O God, will bring those murderers
and liars to their graves
before half their life is over.
As for me, I will trust in you.

A Prayer of Trust in God

56

Be merciful to me, O God,
because I am under attack;
my enemies persecute me all
the time.
²All day long my opponents attack me.
There are so many who fight against me.
³When I am afraid, O LORD Almighty,
I put my trust in you.

**I trust in God
and am not afraid.**

---

⁴I trust in God and am not afraid;
I praise him for what he has promised.
What can a mere human being do to me?

⁵My enemies make trouble for me all day
long;

they are always planning how to hurt me!
⁶They gather in hiding-places
and watch everything I do,
hoping to kill me.
⁷Punish them, O God, for their evil;
defeat those people in your anger!

⁸You know how troubled I am;
you have kept a record of my tears.
Aren't they listed in your book?
⁹The day I call to you,
my enemies will be turned back.
I know this: God is on my side—
¹⁰   the LORD, whose promises I praise.
¹¹In him I trust, and I will not be afraid.
What can a mere human being do to me?

¹²O God, I will offer you what I have promised;
I will give you my offering of thanksgiving,
¹³because you have rescued me from death
and kept me from defeat.
And so I walk in the presence of God,
in the light that shines on the living.

A Prayer for Help

57

Be merciful to me, O God, be
merciful,
because I come to you for
safety.
In the shadow of your wings I find protection
until the raging storms are over.

²I call to God, the Most High,
to God, who supplies my every need.
³He will answer from heaven and save me;
he will defeat my oppressors.
God will show me his constant love and
faithfulness.

⁴I am surrounded by enemies,
who are like man-eating lions,
Their teeth are like spears and arrows;
their tongues are like sharp swords.

⁵Show your greatness in the sky, O God,
and your glory over all the earth.

⁶My enemies have spread a net to catch me;
I am overcome with distress.
They dug a pit in my path,

'Your constant love reaches the heavens; your faithfulness touches the skies.' (Psalm 57.10)

but fell into it themselves.

[7] I have complete confidence, O God;
    I will sing and praise you!
[8] Wake up, my soul!
    Wake up, my harp and lyre!
    I will wake up the sun.
[9] I will thank you, O Lord, among the nations.
    I will praise you among the peoples.
[10] Your constant love reaches the heavens;
    your faithfulness touches the skies.
[11] Show your greatness in the sky, O God,
    and your glory over all the earth.

A Prayer for God to Punish the Wicked

58 Do you rulers ever give a just
        decision?
        Do you judge all men fairly?
[2] No! You think only of the evil you can do,
    and commit crimes of violence in the land.

[3] Evil men go wrong all their lives;
    they tell lies from the day they are born.
[4] They are full of poison like snakes;
    they stop up their ears like a deaf cobra,

[5] which does not hear the voice of the
    snake-charmer,
    or the chant of the clever magician.

[6] Break the teeth of these fierce lions, O God.
[7] May they disappear like water draining
    away;
    may they be crushed like weeds on a path.
[8] May they be like snails that dissolve into
    slime;
    may they be like a baby born dead that
    never sees the light.
[9] Before they know it, they are cut down like
    weeds;
    in his fierce anger God will blow them
    away
    while they are still living.

[10] The righteous will be glad when they see
    sinners punished;
    they will wade through the blood of the
    wicked.
[11] People will say, 'The righteous are indeed
    rewarded;
    there is indeed a God who judges the
    world.'

A Prayer for Safety

59

Save me from my enemies, my
    God
    protect me from those
    who attack me!
²Save me from those evil men;
    rescue me from those murderers!

³Look! They are waiting to kill me;
    cruel men are gathering against me.
It is not because of any sin or wrong I have
    done,
⁴   nor because of any fault of mine, O LORD,
    that they hurry to their places.

⁵Rise, LORD God Almighty, and come to my
    aid;
    see for yourself, God of Israel!
Wake up and punish the heathen;
    show no mercy to evil traitors!

⁶They come back in the evening,
    snarling like dogs as they go about the
    city.
⁷Listen to their insults and threats.
Their tongues are like swords in their
    mouths,
    yet they think that no one hears them.

⁸But you laugh at them, LORD;
    you mock all the heathen.
⁹I have confidence in your strength;
    you are my refuge, O God.

My God loves me and will come to me.

---

¹⁰My God loves me and will come to me;
    he will let me see my enemies defeated.

¹¹Do not kill them, O God, or my people may
    forget.
    Scatter them by your strength and defeat
    them,
    O Lord, our protector.
¹²Sin is on their lips; all their words are sinful;
    may they be caught in their pride!
Because they curse and lie,
¹³   destroy them in your anger;
    destroy them completely.

Then everyone will know that God rules in
    Israel,
    that his rule extends over all the earth.

¹⁴My enemies come back in the evening,
    snarling like dogs as they go about the
    city,
¹⁵   like dogs roaming about for food
    and growling if they do not find enough.

¹⁶But I will sing about your strength;
    every morning I will sing aloud of your
    constant love.
You have been a refuge for me,
    a shelter in my time of trouble.
¹⁷I will praise you, my defender.
    My refuge is God,
    the God who loves me.

A Prayer for Deliverance

60

You have rejected us, God, and
    defeated us;
    you have been angry with us—
    but now turn back to us.
²You have made the land tremble, and you
    have cut it open;
    now heal its wounds, because it is falling
    apart.
³You have made your people suffer greatly;
    we stagger around as though we were
    drunk.
⁴You have warned those who show you
    reverence,
    so that they might escape destruction.
⁵Save us by your might; answer our prayer,
    so that the people you love may be
    rescued.

⁶From his sanctuary God has said,
    'In triumph I will divide Shechem
    and distribute the Valley of Sukkoth to my
    people.
⁷Gilead is mine, and Manasseh too;
    Ephraim is my helmet
    and Judah my royal sceptre.
⁸But I will use Moab as my wash-basin
    and I will throw my sandals on Edom,
    as a sign that I own it.
Did the Philistines think they would shout in
    triumph over me?'

⁹Who, O God, will take me into the fortified
city?
Who will lead me to Edom?
¹⁰Have you really rejected us?
Aren't you going to march out with our
armies?
¹¹Help us against the enemy;
human help is worthless.
¹²With God on our side we will win;
he will defeat our enemies.

A Prayer for Protection

61 Hear my cry, O God;
listen to my prayer!
²In despair and far from home
I call to you!

Take me to a safe refuge,
3 for you are my protector,
my strong defence against my enemies.

⁴Let me live in your sanctuary all my life;
let me find safety under your wings.
⁵You have heard my promises, O God,
and you have given me what belongs to
those who honour you.

⁶Add many years to the king's life;
let him live on and on!
⁷May he rule for ever in your presence, O God;
protect him with your constant love and
faithfulness.

⁸So I will always sing praises to you,
as I offer you daily what I have promised.

Confidence in God's Protection

62 I wait patiently for God to save
me;
I depend on him alone.
²He alone protects and saves me;
he is my defender,
and I shall never be defeated.

³How much longer will all of you attack a man
who is no stronger than a broken-down
fence?
⁴You only want to bring him down from his
place of honour;

'Take me to a safe refuge, for you are my protector ...'
(Psalm 61.2–3)

you take pleasure in lies.
You speak words of blessing,
but in your heart you curse him.

⁵I depend on God alone;
I put my hope in him.
⁶He alone protects and saves me;
he is my defender,
and I shall never be defeated.
⁷My salvation and honour depend on God;
he is my strong protector;
he is my shelter.

⁸Trust in God at all times, my people.
Tell him all your troubles,
for he is our refuge.

Tell him all your troubles ...

---

⁹Men are all like a puff of breath;
great and small alike are worthless.
Put them on the scales, and they weigh
nothing;
they are lighter than a mere breath.
¹⁰Don't put your trust in violence;
don't hope to gain anything by robbery;
even if your riches increase,
don't depend on them.

¹¹More than once I have heard God say
that power belongs to him
12 and that his love is constant.
You yourself, O Lord, reward everyone
according to his deeds.

Longing for God

63 O God, you are my God,
    and I long for you.
    My whole being desires you;
like a dry, worn-out, and waterless land,
    my soul is thirsty for you.
2Let me see you in the sanctuary;
    let me see how mighty and glorious you
    are.
3Your constant love is better than life itself,
    and so I will praise you.
4I will give you thanks as long as I live;
    I will raise my hands to you in prayer.
5My soul will feast and be satisfied,
    and I will sing glad songs of praise to you.

6As I lie in bed, I remember you;
    all night long I think of you,
7   because you have always been my help.
In the shadow of your wings I sing for joy.
8I cling to you,
    and your hand keeps me safe.

9Those who are trying to kill me
    will go down into the world of the dead.
10They will be killed in battle,
    and their bodies eaten by wolves.
11Because God gives him victory,
    the king will rejoice.
Those who make promises in God's name
    will praise him,
    but the mouths of liars will be shut.

A Prayer for Protection

64 I am in trouble, God—listen to my
    prayer!
    I am afraid of my enemies—
    save my life!
2Protect me from the plots of the wicked,
    from mobs of evil men.
3They sharpen their tongues like swords
    and aim cruel words like arrows.
4They are quick to spread their shameless lies;
    they destroy good men with cowardly
    slander.
5They encourage each other in their evil plots;
    they plan where to place their traps.
    'No one can see them,' they say.
6They make evil plans and say,
    'We have planned a perfect crime.'

The heart and mind of man are a mystery.

7But God shoots his arrows at them,
    and suddenly they are wounded.
8He will destroy them because of those
    words;
    all who see them will shake their heads.
9They will all be afraid;
    they will think about what God has done
    and tell about his deeds.
10All righteous people will rejoice
    because of what the LORD has done.
They will find safety in him;
    all good people will praise him.

Praise and Thanksgiving

65 O God, it is right for us to praise
    you in Zion
    and keep our promises to you,
2   because you answer prayers.
People everywhere will come to you
3   on account of their sins.
Our faults defeat us,
    but you forgive them.

**Our faults defeat us,
but you forgive them.**

4Happy are those whom you choose,
    whom you bring to live in your sanctuary.
We shall be satisfied with the good things of
    your house,
    the blessings of your sacred Temple.

5You answer us by giving us victory
    and you do wonderful things to save us.
People all over the world
    and across the distant seas trust in you.
6You set the mountains in place by your
    strength,
    showing your mighty power.
7You calm the roar of the seas
    and the noise of the waves;
    you calm the uproar of the peoples.
8The whole world stands in awe
    of the great things that you have done.
Your deeds bring shouts of joy
    from one end of the earth to the other.

'My whole being desires you; like a dry, worn-out, and waterless land.' (Psalm 63.1) ▷

⁹You show your care for the land by sending
         rain;
      you make it rich and fertile.
   You fill the streams with water;
      you provide the earth with crops.
   This is how you do it:
10   you send abundant rain on the ploughed
         fields
      and soak them with water;
   you soften the soil with showers
      and cause the young plants to grow.
¹¹What a rich harvest your goodness provides!
      Wherever you go there is plenty.

**What a rich harvest
your goodness provides!
Wherever you go there is plenty.**

---

¹²The pastures are filled with flocks;
      the hillsides are full of joy.
¹³The fields are covered with sheep;
      the valleys are full of wheat.
   Everything shouts and sings for joy.

A Song of Praise and Thanksgiving

66 Praise God with shouts of joy, all
         people!
      ²Sing to the glory of his name;
   offer him glorious praise!
³Say to God, 'How wonderful are the things
         you do!
      Your power is so great
      that your enemies bow down in fear
         before you.
⁴Everyone on earth worships you;
      they sing praises to you,
      they sing praises to your name.'

⁵Come and see what God has done,
      his wonderful acts among men.
⁶He changed the sea into dry land;
      our ancestors crossed the river on foot.
   There we rejoiced because of what he did.
⁷He rules for ever by his might
      and keeps his eyes on the nations.
      Let no rebels rise against him.
⁸Praise our God, all nations;
      let your praise be heard.

⁹He has kept us alive
      and has not allowed us to fall.

¹⁰You have put us to the test, God;
      as silver is purified by fire
      so you have tested us.
¹¹You let us fall into a trap
      and placed heavy burdens on our backs.
¹²You let our enemies trample over us;
      we went through fire and flood,
      but now you have brought us to a place of
         safety.

¹³I will bring burnt-offerings to your house;
      I will offer you what I promised.
¹⁴I will give you what I said I would
      when I was in trouble.
¹⁵I will offer sheep to be burnt on the altar;
   I will sacrifice bulls and goats,
      and the smoke will go up to the sky.

¹⁶Come and listen, all who honour God,
      and I will tell you what he has done for me.
¹⁷I cried to him for help;
      I praised him with songs.
¹⁸If I had ignored my sins,
      the Lord would not have listened to me.
¹⁹But God has indeed heard me;
      he has listened to my prayer.

**If I had ignored my sins,
the LORD would not
have listened to me.**

---

²⁰I praise God,
      because he did not reject my prayer
      or keep back his constant love from me.

A Song of Thanksgiving

67 God, be merciful to us and bless us;
         look on us with kindness,
      ²so that the whole world may
         know your will;
   so that all nations may know your
      salvation.

³May the peoples praise you O God;
      may all the peoples praise you!

⁴May the nations be glad and sing for joy,
　　because you judge the peoples with justice
　　and guide every nation on earth.

⁵May the peoples praise you, O God;
　　may all the peoples praise you!

⁶The land has produced its harvest;
　　God, our God, has blessed us.
⁷God has blessed us;
　　may all people everywhere honour him.

A National Song of Triumph

68

God rises up and scatters his
　　enemies.
　　Those who hate him run away
　　in defeat.
²As smoke is blown away, so he drives them
　　off;
　　as wax melts in front of the fire,
　　so do the wicked perish in God's presence.
³But the righteous are glad and rejoice in his
　　presence;
　　they are happy and shout for joy.

**In your goodness
you provided for the poor.**

⁴Sing to God, sing praises to his name;
　　prepare a way for him who rides on the
　　clouds.
　　His name is the LORD—be glad in his
　　presence!

⁵God, who lives in his sacred Temple,
　　cares for orphans and protects widows.
⁶He gives the lonely a home to live in
　　and leads prisoners out into happy
　　freedom,
　　but rebels will have to live in a desolate
　　land.

⁷O God, when you led your people,
　　when you marched across the desert,
⁸the earth shook, and the sky poured down
　　rain,
　　because of the coming of the God of Sinai,
　　the coming of the God of Israel.

⁹You caused abundant rain to fall
　　and restored your worn-out land;
¹⁰your people made their home there;
　　in your goodness you provided for the
　　poor.

¹¹The Lord gave the command,
　　and many women carried the news:
¹²'Kings and their armies are running away!'
　　The women at home divided what was
　　captured:
¹³　figures of doves covered with silver,
　　whose wings glittered with fine gold.
　　(Why did some of you stay among the sheep
　　pens on the day of battle?)
¹⁴When Almighty God scattered the kings on
　　Mount Zalmon,
　　he caused snow to fall there.

¹⁵What a mighty mountain is Bashan,
　　a mountain of many peaks!
¹⁶Why from your mighty peaks do you look
　　with scorn
　　on the mountain on which God chose to
　　live?
　　The LORD will live there for ever!

¹⁷With his many thousands of mighty chariots
　　the Lord comes from Sinai into the holy
　　place.
¹⁸He goes up to the heights,
　　taking many captives with him;
　　he receives gifts from rebellious men.
　　The LORD God will live there.

¹⁹Praise the Lord,
　　who carries our burdens day after day;

**Praise the LORD,
who carries our burdens ...**

　　he is the God who saves us.
²⁰Our God is a God who saves;
　　he is the LORD, our Lord,
　　who rescues us from death.

²¹God will surely break the heads of his
　　enemies,
　　of those who persist in their sinful ways.

²²The Lord has said, 'I will bring your enemies
back from Bashan;
I will bring them back from the depths of
the ocean,
²³so that you may wade in their blood,
and your dogs may lap up as much as they
want.'

²⁴O God, your march of triumph is seen by all,
the procession of God, my king, into his
sanctuary.
²⁵The singers are in front, the musicians are
behind,
in between are the girls beating the
tambourines.
²⁶'Praise God in the meeting of his people;
praise the LORD, all you descendants of
Jacob!'

Show your power, O God ...

²⁷First comes Benjamin, the smallest tribe,
then the leaders of Judah with their
group,
followed by the leaders of Zebulun and
Naphtali.

²⁸Show your power, O God,
the power you have used on our behalf
²⁹   from your Temple in Jerusalem,
where kings bring gifts to you.
³⁰Rebuke Egypt, that wild animal in the reeds;
rebuke the nations, that herd of bulls with
their calves,
until they all bow down and offer you
their silver.
Scatter those people who love to make war!
³¹Ambassadors will come from Egypt;
the Sudanese will raise their hands in
prayer to God.

³²Sing to God, kingdoms of the world,
sing praise to the Lord,
³³   to him who rides in the sky,
the ancient sky.
Listen to him shout with a mighty roar.
³⁴Proclaim God's power;
his majesty is over Israel,
his might is in the skies.

³⁵How awesome is God as he comes from his
sanctuary—
the God of Israel!
He gives strength and power to his people.

Praise God!

A Cry for Help

69
Save me, O God!
The water is up to my neck;
²I am sinking in deep mud,
and there is no solid ground;
I am out in deep water,
and the waves are about to drown me.
³I am worn out from calling for help,
and my throat is aching.
I have strained my eyes,
looking for your help.

⁴Those who hate me for no reason
are more numerous than the hairs of my
head.
My enemies tell lies against me;
they are strong and want to kill me.
They made me give back things I did not
steal.
⁵My sins, O God, are not hidden from you;
you know how foolish I have been.
⁶Don't let me bring shame on those who trust
in you,
Sovereign LORD Almighty!
Don't let me bring disgrace to those who
worship you,
O God of Israel!
⁷It is for your sake that I have been insulted
and that I am covered with shame.

The insults
which are hurled at you
fall on me.

⁸I am like a stranger to my brothers,
like a foreigner to my family.

⁹My devotion to your Temple burns in me like
a fire;
the insults which are hurled at you fall on
me.

¹⁰I humble myself by fasting,
and people insult me;
¹¹I dress myself in clothes of mourning,
and they laugh at me.
¹²They talk about me in the streets,
and drunkards make up songs about me.

¹³But as for me, I will pray to you, LORD;
answer me, God, at a time you choose.

Answer me, God,
at a time you choose.

Answer me because of your great love,
because you keep your promise to save.
¹⁴Save me from sinking in the mud;
keep me safe from my enemies,
safe from the deep water.
¹⁵Don't let the flood come over me;
don't let me drown in the depths
or sink into the grave.

¹⁶Answer me, LORD, in the goodness of your
constant love;
in your great compassion turn to me!
¹⁷Don't hide yourself from your servant;
I am in great trouble—answer me now!
¹⁸Come to me and save me;
rescue me from my enemies.

¹⁹You know how I am insulted,
how I am disgraced and dishonoured;
you see all my enemies.
²⁰Insults have broken my heart,
and I am in despair.
I had hoped for sympathy, but there was
none;
for comfort, but I found none.
²¹When I was hungry, they gave me poison;
when I was thirsty, they offered me
vinegar.
²²May their banquets cause their ruin;
may their sacred feasts cause their
downfall.
²³Strike them with blindness!

'I am out in deep water ...' (Psalm 69.2)

Make their backs always weak!
²⁴Pour out your anger on them;
    let your indignation overtake them.
²⁵May their camps be left deserted;
    may no one be left alive in their tents.
²⁶They persecute those whom you have
      punished;
    they talk about the sufferings of those
      you have wounded.
²⁷Keep a record of all their sins;
    don't let them have any part in your
      salvation.
²⁸May their names be erased from the book of
      the living;
    may they not be included in the list of your
      people.

²⁹But I am in pain and despair;
    lift me up, O God, and save me!

³⁰I will praise God with a song;
    I will proclaim his greatness by giving him
      thanks.
³¹This will please the LORD more than offering
      him cattle,
    more than sacrificing a full-grown bull.
³²When the oppressed see this, they will be
      glad;
    those who worship God will be
      encouraged.
³³The LORD listens to those in need
    and does not forget his people in prison.

³⁴Praise God, O heaven and earth,
    seas and all creatures in them.
³⁵He will save Jerusalem
    and rebuild the towns of Judah.
His people will live there and possess the
      land;
³⁶ the descendants of his servants will
      inherit it,
    and those who love him will live there.

A Prayer for Help

70 Save me, O God!
    LORD, help me now!
    ²May those who try to kill me
be defeated and confused.
May those who are happy because of my
   troubles

be turned back and disgraced.
³May those who jeer at me
    be dismayed by their defeat.

⁴May all who come to you
    be glad and joyful.
May all who are thankful for your salvation
    always say, 'How great is God!'

⁵I am weak and poor;
    come to me quickly, O God.
You are my saviour, O LORD—
    hurry to my aid!

An Old Man's Prayer

71 LORD, I have come to you for
      protection;
      never let me be defeated!
²Because you are righteous, help me and
    rescue me.
Listen to me and save me!
³Be my secure shelter
    and a strong fortress to protect me;
    you are my refuge and defence.

⁴My God, rescue me from wicked men,
    from the power of cruel and evil men.

**I have trusted
in you
since I was young.**

---

⁵Sovereign LORD, I put my hope in you;
    I have trusted in you since I was young.
⁶I have relied on you all my life;
    you have protected me since the day I was
      born.
    I will always praise you.

⁷My life has been an example to many,
    because you have been my strong
      defender.
⁸All day long I praise you
    and proclaim your glory.
⁹Do not reject me now that I am old;
    do not abandon me now that I am feeble.
¹⁰My enemies want to kill me;
    they talk and plot against me.

[11] They say, 'God has abandoned him;
    let's go after him and catch him;
    there is no one to rescue him.'

[12] Don't stay so far away, O God;
    my God, hurry to my aid!

Don't stay so far
away, O God.

---

[13] May those who attack me
    be defeated and destroyed.
  May those who try to hurt me
    be shamed and disgraced.
[14] I will always put my hope in you;
    I will praise you more and more.
[15] I will tell of your goodness;
    all day long I will speak of your salvation,
    though it is more than I can understand.
[16] I will praise your power, Sovereign LORD;
    I will proclaim your goodness, yours alone.

[17] You have taught me ever since I was young,
    and I still tell of your wonderful acts.
[18] Now that I am old and my hair is grey,
    do not abandon me, O God!
  Be with me while I proclaim your power and
      might
    to all generations to come.

[19] Your righteousness, God, reaches the skies.
    You have done great things;
    there is no one like you.
[20] You have sent troubles and suffering on me,
    but you will restore my strength;
    you will keep me from the grave.

You will comfort me again.

---

[21] You will make me greater than ever;
    you will comfort me again.

[22] I will indeed praise you with the harp;
    I will praise your faithfulness, my God.
  On my harp I will play hymns to you,
    the Holy One of Israel.
[23] I will shout for joy as I play for you;

with my whole being I will sing
    because you have saved me.
[24] I will speak of your righteousness all day
      long,
    because those who tried to harm me
    have been defeated and disgraced.

A Prayer for the King

72
Teach the king to judge with your
    righteousness, O God;
    share with him your own
    justice,
[2] so that he will rule over your people with
      justice
    and govern the oppressed with
    righteousness.
[3] May the land enjoy prosperity;
    may it experience righteousness.
[4] May the king judge the poor fairly;
    may he help the needy
    and defeat their oppressors.
[5] May your people worship you as long as the
      sun shines,
    as long as the moon gives light, for ages to
    come.

[6] May the king be like rain on the fields,
    like showers falling on the land.

May righteousness flourish ...
and may prosperity last
as long as the moon gives light.

---

[7] May righteousness flourish in his lifetime,
    and may prosperity last as long as the
    moon gives light.

[8] His kingdom will reach from sea to sea,
    from the Euphrates to the ends of the
    earth.
[9] The peoples of the desert will bow down
      before him;
    his enemies will throw themselves to the
    ground.
[10] The kings of Spain and of the islands will
    offer him gifts;
    the kings of Sheba and Seba will bring him
    offerings.

¹¹All kings will bow down before him;
　　all nations will serve him.

¹²He rescues the poor who call to him,
　　and those who are needy and neglected.
¹³He has pity on the weak and poor;
　　he saves the lives of those in need.
¹⁴He rescues them from oppression and
　　violence;
　　their lives are precious to him.

¹⁵Long live the king!
　　May he be given gold from Sheba;
　　may prayers be said for him at all times;
　　may God's blessings be on him always!
¹⁶May there be plenty of corn in the land;
　　may the hills be covered with crops,
　　as fruitful as those of Lebanon.
　May the cities be filled with people,
　　like fields full of grass.
¹⁷May the king's name never be forgotten;
　　may his fame last as long as the sun.
　May all nations ask God to bless them
　　as he has blessed the king.

¹⁸Praise the LORD, the God of Israel!
　He alone does these wonderful things.
¹⁹Praise his glorious name for ever!
　May his glory fill the whole world.

Amen! Amen!

²⁰This is the end of the prayers of David son of
　　Jesse.

BOOK THREE
(Psalms 73–89)

The Justice of God

73
God is indeed good to Israel,
　　to those who have pure hearts.
²But I had nearly lost confidence;
　my faith was almost gone
³because I was jealous of the proud
　　when I saw that things go well for the
　　wicked.

⁴They do not suffer pain;
　　they are strong and healthy.
⁵They do not suffer as other people do;

they do not have the troubles that others
　　have.
⁶And so they wear pride like a necklace
　　and violence like a robe;
⁷their hearts pour out evil,
　　and their minds are busy with wicked
　　schemes.
⁸They laugh at other people and speak of evil
　　things;
　　they are proud and make plans to oppress
　　others.
⁹They speak evil of God in heaven
　　and give arrogant orders to men on earth,
¹⁰so that even God's people turn to them
　　and eagerly believe whatever they say.

**They speak evil of God in heaven
and give arrogant orders
to men on earth.**

---

¹¹They say, 'God will not know;
　　the Most High will not find out.'
¹²That is what the wicked are like.
　　They have plenty and are always getting
　　more.

¹³Is it for nothing, then, that I have kept
　　myself pure
　　and have not committed sin?
¹⁴O God, you have made me suffer all day long;
　　every morning you have punished me.

¹⁵If I had said such things,
　　I would not be acting as one of your
　　people.
¹⁶I tried to think this problem through,
　　but it was too difficult for me
¹⁷　Until I went into your Temple.

**Then I understood
what will happen to the wicked.**

Then I understood what will happen to the
　　wicked.

¹⁸You will put them in slippery places
　　and make them fall to destruction!

'He has pity on the weak and poor ...' (Psalm 72.13) ▷

¹⁹They are instantly destroyed;
  they go down to a horrible end.
²⁰They are like a dream that goes away in the
    morning;
  when you rouse yourself, O Lord, they
    disappear.

²¹When my thoughts were bitter
  and my feelings were hurt,
²²I was as stupid as an animal;
  I did not understand you.
²³Yet I always stay close to you,
  and you hold me by the hand.
²⁴You guide me with your instruction
  and at the end you will receive me with
    honour.
²⁵What else have I in heaven but you?
  Since I have you, what else could I want on
    earth?
²⁶My mind and my body may grow weak,
  but God is my strength;
  he is all I ever need.

²⁷Those who abandon you will certainly perish;
  you will destroy those who are unfaithful
    to you.

... how wonderful to be near God, to find protection with the Sovereign LORD ...

---

²⁸But as for me, how wonderful to be near
    God,
  to find protection with the Sovereign LORD
  and to proclaim all that he has done!

A Prayer for National Deliverance

74
Why have you abandoned us like
    this, O God?
  Will you be angry with your
    own people for ever?
²Remember your people, whom you chose
  for yourself long ago,
  whom you brought out of slavery to be
    your own tribe.
  Remember Mount Zion, where once you
    lived.
³Walk over these total ruins;

our enemies have destroyed everything in
    the Temple.

⁴Your enemies have shouted in triumph in
    your Temple;
  they have placed their flags there as signs
    of victory.

How long, O God, will our enemies laugh at you?

---

⁵They looked like woodmen
  cutting down trees with their axes.
⁶They smashed all the wooden panels
  with their axes and sledge-hammers.
⁷They wrecked your Temple and set it on fire;
  they desecrated the place where you are
    worshipped.
⁸They wanted to crush us completely;
  they burnt down every holy place in the
    land.

⁹All our sacred symbols are gone;
  there are no prophets left,
  and no one knows how long this will last.
¹⁰How long, O God, will our enemies laugh at
    you?
  Will they insult your name for ever?
¹¹Why have you refused to help us?
  Why do you keep your hands behind you?

¹²But you have been our king from the
    beginning, O God;
  you have saved us many times.
¹³With your mighty strength you divided the
    sea
  and smashed the heads of the sea-
    monsters;
¹⁴you crushed the heads of the monster
    Leviathan
  and fed his body to desert animals.
¹⁵You made springs and fountains flow;
  you dried up large rivers.
¹⁶You created the day and the night;
  you set the sun and the moon in their
    places;
¹⁷you set the limits of the earth;
  you made summer and winter.

[18]But remember, O Lord, that your enemies
laugh at you,
that they are godless and despise you.
[19]Don't abandon your helpless people to their
cruel enemies;
don't forget your persecuted people!

[20]Remember the covenant you made with us.
There is violence in every dark corner of
the land.
[21]Don't let the oppressed be put to shame;
let those poor and needy people praise
you.

[22]Rouse yourself, God, and defend your cause!
Remember that godless people laugh at
you all day long.
[23]Don't forget the angry shouts of your
enemies,
the continuous noise made by your foes.

God the Judge

75 We give thanks to you, O God, we
give thanks to you!
We proclaim how great you are
and tell of the wonderful things you have
done.

[2]'I have set a time for judgement,' says God,
'and I will judge with fairness.
[3]Though every living creature tremble
and the earth itself be shaken,
I will keep its foundations firm.
[4]I tell the wicked not to be arrogant;
[5] I tell them to stop their boasting.'

[6]Judgement does not come from the east or
from the west,
from the north or from the south;
[7]it is God who is the judge,

'... I will judge with fairness.'

---

condemning some and acquitting others.
[8]The Lord holds a cup in his hand,
filled with the strong wine of his anger.
He pours it out, and all the wicked drink it;
they drink it down to the last drop.

[9]But I will never stop speaking of the God of
Jacob
or singing praises to him.
[10]He will break the power of the wicked,
but the power of the righteous will be
increased.

God the Victor

76 God is known in Judah;
his name is honoured in Israel.
[2]He has his home in Jerusalem;
he lives on Mount Zion.
[3]There he broke the arrows of the enemy,
their shields and swords, yes, all their
weapons.

[4]How glorious you are, O God!
How majestic, as you return from the
mountains
where you defeated your foes.
[5]Their brave soldiers have been stripped of all
they had
and now are sleeping the sleep of death;
all their strength and skill was useless.
[6]When you threatened them, O God of Jacob,
the horses and their riders fell dead.

[7]But you, Lord, are feared by all.
No one can stand in your presence
when you are angry.

... you rose up
to pronounce judgement,
to save all the oppressed ...

---

[8]You made your judgement known from
heaven;
the world was afraid and kept silent,
[9]when you rose up to pronounce judgement,
to save all the oppressed on earth.

[10]Men's anger only results in more praise for
you;
those who survive the wars will keep your
festivals.

[11]Give the Lord your God what you promised
him;

*You have taught me
ever since I was young,
and I still tell of your
wonderful acts.*

Psalm 71.17

bring gifts to him, all you nearby nations.
God makes men fear him;
12   he humbles proud princes
      and terrifies great kings.

Comfort in Time of Distress

77

I cry aloud to God;
        I cry aloud, and he hears me.
    ²In times of trouble I pray to the
        Lord;
all night long I lift my hands in prayer,
    but I cannot find comfort.
³When I think of God, I sigh;
    when I meditate, I feel discouraged.

⁴He keeps me awake all night;
    I am so worried that I cannot speak.
⁵I think of days gone by
    and remember years of long ago.
⁶I spend the night in deep thought;
    I meditate, and this is what I ask myself:
⁷'Will the Lord always reject us?
    Will he never again be pleased with us?
⁸Has he stopped loving us?
    Does his promise no longer stand?
⁹Has God forgotten to be merciful?
    Has anger taken the place of his
        compassion?'
¹⁰Then I said, 'What hurts me most is this—
    that God is no longer powerful.'

¹¹I will remember your great deeds, LORD;
    I will recall the wonders you did in the
        past.
¹²I will think about all that you have done;
    I will meditate on all your mighty acts.

¹³Everything you do, O God, is holy.
    No god is as great as you.

You are the God
who works miracles.

¹⁴You are the God who works miracles;
    you showed your might among the
        nations.
¹⁵By your power you saved your people,
    the descendants of Jacob and of Joseph.

¹⁶When the waters saw you, O God, they were
        afraid,
    and the depths of the sea trembled.
¹⁷The clouds poured down rain;
    thunder crashed from the sky,
    and lightning flashed in all directions.
¹⁸The crash of your thunder rolled out,
    and flashes of lightning lit up the world;
    the earth trembled and shook.
¹⁹You walked through the waves;
    you crossed the deep sea,
    but your footprints could not be seen.
²⁰You led your people like a shepherd,
    with Moses and Aaron in charge.

God and His People

78

Listen, my people, to my teaching,
        and pay attention to what I say.
    ²I am going to use wise sayings
and explain mysteries from the past,
3   things we have heard and known,
    things that our fathers told us.
⁴We will not keep them from our children;
    we will tell the next generation

We will tell
the next generation
about the LORD's power ...

about the LORD's power and his great
    deeds
and the wonderful things he has done.

⁵He gave laws to the people of Israel
    and commandments to the descendants
        of Jacob.
He instructed our ancestors
    to teach his laws to their children,
⁶so that the next generation might learn them
    and in turn should tell their children.
⁷In this way they also would put their trust in
        God
    and not forget what he has done,
    but always obey his commandments.
⁸They would not be like their ancestors,
    a rebellious and disobedient people,
whose trust in God was never firm
    and who did not remain faithful to him.

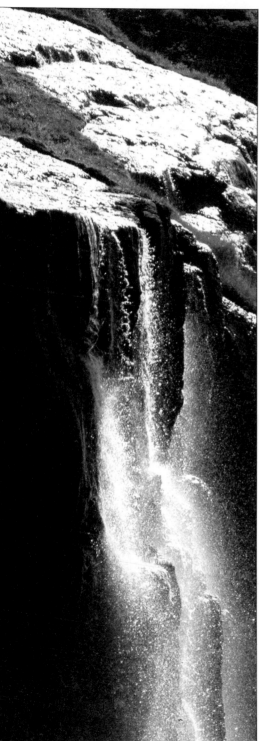

⁹The Ephraimites, armed with bows and
arrows,
ran away on the day of battle.
¹⁰They did not keep their covenant with God;
they refused to obey his law.
¹¹They forgot what he had done,
the miracles they had seen him perform.
¹²While their ancestors watched, God
performed miracles
in the plain of Zoan in the land of Egypt.
¹³He divided the sea and took them through it;
he made the waters stand like walls.
¹⁴By day he led them with a cloud
and all night long with the light of a fire.
¹⁵He split rocks open in the desert
and gave them water from the depths.
¹⁶He caused a stream to come out of the rock
and made water flow like a river.

¹⁷But they continued to sin against God,
and in the desert they rebelled against the
Most High.

... they continued to sin against God ...

---

¹⁸They deliberately put God to the test
by demanding the food they wanted.
¹⁹They spoke against God and said,
'Can God supply food in the desert?
²⁰It is true that he struck the rock,
and water flowed out in a torrent;
but can he also provide us with bread
and give his people meat?'

²¹And so the LORD was angry when he heard
them;
he attacked his people with fire,
and his anger against them grew,
²²because they had no faith in him
and did not believe that he would save them.
²³But he spoke to the sky above
and commanded its doors to open;
²⁴he gave them grain from heaven,
by sending down manna for them to eat.
²⁵So they ate the food of angels,
and God gave them all they wanted.
²⁶He also caused the east wind to blow,
and by his power he stirred up the south
wind;

'He caused a stream to come out of the rock ...' (Psalm 78.16)

²⁷and to his people he sent down birds,
 as many as the grains of sand on the shore;
²⁸they fell in the middle of the camp
 all round the tents.
²⁹So the people ate and were satisfied;
 God gave them what they wanted.
³⁰But they had not yet satisfied their craving
 and were still eating,
³¹when God became angry with them
 and killed their strongest men,
 the best young men of Israel.

³²In spite of all this the people kept sinning;
 in spite of his miracles they did not trust
 him.

**They were not loyal to him;
they were not faithful
to their covenant with him.**

---

³³So he ended their days like a breath
 and their lives with sudden disaster.
³⁴Whenever he killed some of them,
 the rest would turn to him;
 they would repent and pray earnestly to
 him.
³⁵They remembered that God was their
 protector,
 that the Almighty came to their aid.
³⁶But their words were all lies;
 nothing they said was sincere.
³⁷They were not loyal to him;
 they were not faithful to their covenant
 with him.

³⁸But God was merciful to his people.
 He forgave their sin
 and did not destroy them.
 Many times he held back his anger
 and restrained his fury.
³⁹He remembered that they were only mortal
 beings,
 like a wind that blows by and is gone.

⁴⁰How often they rebelled against him in the
 desert;
 how many times they made him sad!
⁴¹Again and again they put God to the test
 and brought pain to the Holy God of Israel.

⁴²They forgot his great power
 and the day when he saved them from
 their enemies
⁴³   and performed his mighty acts and
 miracles
 in the plain of Zoan in the land of Egypt.
⁴⁴He turned the rivers into blood,
 and the Egyptians had no water to drink.
⁴⁵He sent flies among them, that tormented
 them,
 and frogs that ruined their land.
⁴⁶He sent locusts to eat their crops
 and to destroy their fields.
⁴⁷He killed their grapevines with hail
 and their fig-trees with frost.
⁴⁸He killed their cattle with hail
 and their flocks with lightning.
⁴⁹He caused them great distress
 by pouring out his anger and fierce rage,
 which came as messengers of death.
⁵⁰He did not restrain his anger
 or spare their lives,
 but killed them with a plague.
⁵¹He killed the first-born sons
 of all the families of Egypt.

⁵²Then he led his people out like a shepherd
 and guided them through the desert.
⁵³He led them safely, and they were not afraid;
 but the sea came rolling over their
 enemies.
⁵⁴He brought them to his holy land,
 to the mountains which he himself
 conquered.

**He led them safely,
and they were not afraid.**

---

⁵⁵He drove out the inhabitants as his people
 advanced;
 he divided their land among the tribes of
 Israel
 and gave their homes to his people.

⁵⁶But they rebelled against Almighty God
 and put him to the test.
 They did not obey his commandments,
⁵⁷   but were rebellious and disloyal like their
 fathers,

unreliable as a crooked arrow.
[58]They angered him with their heathen places
of worship,
and with their idols they made him
furious.
[59]God was angry when he saw it,
so he rejected his people completely.
[60]He abandoned his tent in Shiloh,
the home where he had lived among us.
[61]He allowed our enemies to capture the
Covenant Box,
the symbol of his power and glory.

**He was angry with
his own people and let them
be killed by their enemies.**

---

[62]He was angry with his own people
and let them be killed by their enemies.
[63]Young men were killed in war,
and young women had no one to marry.
[64]Priests died by violence,
and their widows were not allowed to
mourn.

[65]At last the Lord woke up as though from
sleep;
he was like a strong man excited by
wine.
[66]He drove his enemies back
in lasting and shameful defeat.
[67]But he rejected the descendants of
Joseph;
he did not select the tribe of Ephraim.
[68]Instead he chose the tribe of Judah
and Mount Zion, which he dearly loves.
[69]There he built his Temple
like his home in heaven;
he made it firm like the earth itself,
secure for all time.

[70]He chose his servant David;
he took him from the pastures,
[71]   where he looked after his flocks,
and made him king of Israel,
the shepherd of the people of God.
[72]David took care of them with unselfish
devotion
and led them with skill.

A Prayer for the Nation's Deliverance

79 O God, the heathen have invaded
your land.
They have desecrated your
holy Temple
and left Jerusalem in ruins.
[2]They left the bodies of your people for the
vultures,
the bodies of your servants for wild
animals to eat.
[3]They shed your people's blood like water;
blood flowed like water all through
Jerusalem,
and no one was left to bury the dead.
[4]The surrounding nations insult us;
they laugh at us and mock us.

[5]LORD, will you be angry with us for ever?
Will your anger continue to burn like fire?
[6]Turn your anger on the nations that do not
worship you,
on the people who do not pray to you.
[7]For they have killed your people;
they have ruined your country.

[8]Do not punish us for the sins of our
ancestors.
Have mercy on us now;
we have lost all hope.
[9]Help us, O God, and save us;
rescue us and forgive our sins
for the sake of your own honour.

Help us, O God, and save us.

---

[10]Why should the nations ask us,
'Where is your God?'
Let us see you punish the nations
for shedding the blood of your servants.

[11]Listen to the groans of the prisoners,
and by your great power free those who
are condemned to die.
[12]Lord, pay the other nations back seven times
for all the insults they have hurled at you.
[13]Then we, your people, the sheep of your
flock,
will thank you for ever
and praise you for all time to come.

A Prayer for the Nation's Restoration

80 Listen to us, O Shepherd of Israel;
hear us, leader of your flock.
Seated on your throne above the
winged creatures,
2   reveal yourself to the tribes of Ephraim,
Benjamin, and Manasseh.
Show us your strength;
come and save us!

3Bring us back, O God!
Show us your mercy, and we will be saved!

4How much longer, LORD God Almighty,
will you be angry with your people's
prayers?
5You have given us sorrow to eat,
a large cup of tears to drink.

Bring us back, Almighty God!

6You let the surrounding nations fight over
our land;
our enemies insult us.

7Bring us back, Almighty God!
Show us your mercy, and we will be saved!

8You brought a grapevine out of Egypt;
you drove out other nations and planted it
in their land.
9You cleared a place for it to grow;
its roots went deep, and it spread out over
the whole land.
10It covered the hills with its shade;
its branches overshadowed the giant
cedars.
11It extended its branches to the
Mediterranean Sea
and as far as the River Euphrates.
12Why did you break down the fences round
it?
Now anyone passing by can steal its
grapes;
13   wild pigs trample it down,
and wild animals feed on it.

14Turn to us, Almighty God!
Look down from heaven at us;

come and save your people!
15Come and save this grapevine that you
planted,
this young vine you made grow so strong!

16Our enemies have set it on fire and cut it
down;
look at them in anger and destroy them!
17Preserve and protect the people you have
chosen,
the nation you made so strong.
18We will never turn away from you again;
keep us alive, and we will praise you.

19Bring us back, LORD God Almighty.
Show us your mercy, and we will be saved.

A Song for a Festival

81 Shout for joy to God our
defender;
sing praise to the God of Jacob!
2Start the music and beat the tambourines;
play pleasant music on the harps and the
lyres.
3Blow the trumpet for the festival,
when the moon is new and when the
moon is full.
4This is the law in Israel,
an order from the God of Jacob.
5He gave it to the people of Israel
when he attacked the land of Egypt.

I hear an unknown voice saying,
6'I took the burdens off your backs;
I let you put down your loads of bricks.
7When you were in trouble, you called to me,
and I saved you.
From my hiding-place in the storm, I
answered you.
I put you to the test at the springs of
Meribah.
8Listen, my people, to my warning;
Israel, how I wish you would listen to me!
9You must never worship another god.
10I am the LORD your God,
who brought you out of Egypt.
Open your mouth, and I will feed you.

11'But my people would not listen to me;
Israel would not obey me.

'Start the music and beat the tambourines ... blow the trumpet for the festival.' (Psalm 81.2–3)

¹²So I let them go their stubborn ways
and do whatever they wanted.
¹³How I wish my people would listen to me;
how I wish they would obey me!
¹⁴I would quickly defeat their enemies
and conquer all their foes.
¹⁵Those who hate me would bow in fear
before me;
their punishment would last for ever.
¹⁶But I would feed you with the finest wheat
and satisfy you with wild honey.'

God the Supreme Ruler

82 God presides in the heavenly
council;
in the assembly of the gods he
gives his decision:
²'You must stop judging unjustly;
you must no longer be partial to the
wicked!
³Defend the rights of the poor and the
orphans;
be fair to the needy and the helpless.
⁴Rescue them from the power of evil men.

**Come, O God, and rule the world;
all the nations are yours.**

---

⁵'How ignorant you are! How stupid!
You are completely corrupt,
and justice has disappeared from the
world.
⁶"You are gods," I said;
"all of you are sons of the Most High."
⁷But you will die like men;
your life will end like that of any prince.'

⁸Come, O God, and rule the world;
all the nations are yours.

A Prayer for the Defeat of Israel's Enemies

83 O God, do not keep silent;
do not be still, do not be quiet!
²Look! Your enemies are in revolt,
and those who hate you are rebelling.
³They are making secret plans against your
people;

they are plotting against those you protect.
⁴'Come,' they say, 'let us destroy their nation,
so that Israel will be forgotten for ever.'

⁵They agree on their plan
and form an alliance against you:
⁶the people of Edom and the Ishmaelites;
the people of Moab and the Hagrites;
⁷the people of Gebal, Ammon, and Amalek,
and of Philistia and Tyre.
⁸Assyria has also joined them
as a strong ally of the Ammonites and
Moabites, the descendants of Lot.

⁹Do to them what you did to the Midianites,
and to Sisera and Jabin at the River
Kishon.
¹⁰You defeated them at Endor,
and their bodies rotted on the ground.
¹¹Do to their leaders what you did to Oreb and
Zeeb;
defeat all their rulers as you did Zebah
and Zalmunna,
¹²who said, 'We will take for our own
the land that belongs to God.'

¹³Scatter them like dust, O God,
like straw blown away by the wind.
¹⁴As fire burns the forest,
as flames set the hills on fire,
¹⁵chase them away with your storm
and terrify them with your fierce winds.
¹⁶Cover their faces with shame, O LORD,
and make them acknowledge your power.
¹⁷May they be defeated and terrified for ever;
may they die in complete disgrace.
¹⁸May they know that you alone are the LORD,
supreme ruler over all the earth.

Longing for God's House

84 How I love your Temple, LORD
Almighty!
² How I want to be there!
I long to be in the LORD's Temple.
With my whole being I sing for joy
to the living God.
³Even the sparrows have built a nest,
and the swallows have their own home;
they keep their young near your altars,
LORD Almighty, my king and my God.

[4]How happy are those who live in your
Temple,
always singing praise to you.

[5]How happy are those whose strength comes
from you,
who are eager to make the pilgrimage
to Mount Zion.
[6]As they pass through the dry valley of Baca,
it becomes a place of springs;
the autumn rain fills it with pools.
[7]They grow stronger as they go;
they will see the God of gods on Zion.

[8]Hear my prayer, LORD God Almighty.
Listen, O God of Jacob!
[9]Bless our king, O God,
the king you have chosen.

[10]One day spent in your Temple
is better than a thousand anywhere else;

**One day spent in your Temple
is better than
a thousand anywhere else.**

I would rather stand at the gate of the house
of my God
than live in the homes of the wicked.
[11]The LORD is our protector and glorious king,
blessing us with kindness and honour.
He does not refuse any good thing
to those who do what is right.
[12]LORD Almighty, how happy are those who
trust in you!

A Prayer for the Nation's Welfare

85

LORD, you have been merciful to
your land;
you have made Israel
prosperous again.
[2]You have forgiven your people's sins
and pardoned all their wrongs.
[3]You stopped being angry with them
and held back your furious rage.

[4]Bring us back, O God our sáviour,
and stop being displeased with us!

[5]Will you be angry with us for ever?
Will your anger never cease?
[6]Make us strong again,
and we, your people, will praise you.
[7]Show us your constant love, O LORD,
and give us your saving help.

[8]I am listening to what the LORD God is saying;
he promises peace to us, his own people,
if we do not go back to our foolish ways.

**He promises peace to us ...
if we do not go back
to our foolish ways.**

---

[9]Surely he is ready to save those who honour
him,
and his saving presence will remain in our
land.

[10]Love and faithfulness will meet;
righteousness and peace will embrace.
[11]Man's loyalty will reach up from the earth,
and God's righteousness will look down
from heaven.
[12]The LORD will make us prosperous,
and our land will produce rich harvests.
[13]Righteousness will go before the LORD
and prepare the path for him.

A Prayer for Help

86

Listen to me, LORD, and answer me,
for I am helpless and weak.
[2]Save me from death, because I
am loyal to you;
save me, for I am your servant and I trust
in you.

[3]You are my God, so be merciful to me;
I pray to you all day long.
[4]Make your servant glad, O Lord,
because my prayers go up to you.
[5]You are good to us and forgiving,
full of constant love for all who pray to
you.

[6]Listen, LORD, to my prayer;
hear my cries for help.

[7]I call to you in times of trouble,
    because you answer my prayers.

[8]There is no god like you, O LORD,
    not one has done what you have done.

**Teach me, LORD,
what you want me to do ...**

---

[9]All the nations that you have created
    will come and bow down to you;
    they will praise your greatness.
[10]You are mighty and do wonderful things;
    you alone are God.

[11]Teach me, LORD, what you want me to do,
    and I will obey you faithfully;
    teach me to serve you with complete
      devotion.
[12]I will praise you with all my heart, O Lord my
      God;
    I will proclaim your greatness for ever.
[13]How great is your constant love for me!
    You have saved me from the grave itself.
[14]Proud men are coming against me, O God;
    a gang of cruel men is trying to kill me—
    people who pay no attention to you.
[15]But you, O Lord, are a merciful and loving
      God,
    always patient, always kind and faithful.
[16]Turn to me and have mercy on me;
    strengthen me and save me,
    because I serve you, just as my mother did.
[17]Show me proof of your goodness, LORD;
    those who hate me will be ashamed
    when they see that you have given me
    comfort and help.

In Praise of Jerusalem

87 The LORD built his city on the
          sacred hill;
    [2] more than any other place in
          Israel
    he loves the city of Jerusalem.
[3]Listen, city of God,
    to the wonderful things he says about you:

⌐I will include Egypt and Babylonia

when I list the nations that obey me;
I will number among the inhabitants of
    Jerusalem
    the people of Philistia, Tyre, and Sudan.'

[5]Of Zion it will be said
    that all nations belong there
    and that the Almighty will make her
      strong.
[6]The LORD will write a list of the peoples
    and include them all as citizens of
      Jerusalem.
[7]They dance and sing,
    'In Zion is the source of all our blessings.'

A Cry for Help

88 LORD God, my saviour, I cry out all
          day,
          and at night I come before you.
[2]Hear my prayer;
    listen to my cry for help!

[3]So many troubles have fallen on me
    that I am close to death.
[4]I am like all others who are about to die;
    all my strength is gone.
[5]I am abandoned among the dead;
    I am like the slain lying in their graves,
    those you have forgotten completely,
    who are beyond your help.

LORD, every day I call to you ...

---

[6]You have thrown me into the depths of the
      tomb,
    into the darkest and deepest pit.
[7]Your anger lies heavy on me,
    and I am crushed beneath its waves.

[8]You have caused my friends to abandon me;
    you have made me repulsive to them.
I am closed in and cannot escape;
[9] my eyes are weak from suffering.
LORD, every day I call to you
    and lift my hands to you in prayer.

[10]Do you perform miracles for the dead?
    Do they rise up and praise you?

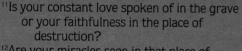

¹¹Is your constant love spoken of in the grave
    or your faithfulness in the place of
    destruction?
¹²Are your miracles seen in that place of
    darkness
    or your goodness in the land of the
    forgotten?

¹³LORD, I call to you for help;
    every morning I pray to you.
¹⁴Why do you reject me, LORD?
    Why do you turn away from me?
¹⁵Ever since I was young, I have suffered and
    been near death;
    I am worn out from the burden of your
    punishments.
¹⁶Your furious anger crushes me;
    your terrible attacks destroy me.
¹⁷All day long they surround me like a flood;
    they close in on me from every side.
¹⁸You have made even my closest friends
    abandon me,
    and darkness is my only companion.

A Hymn in Time of National Trouble

89 O LORD, I will always sing of your
    constant love;
    I will proclaim your faithfulness
    for ever.
²I know that your love will last for all time,
    that your faithfulness is as permanent as
    the sky.

**... your love will last for all time ...
your faithfulness
is as permanent as the sky.**

---

³You said, 'I have made a covenant with the
    man I chose;
    I have promised my servant David,
⁴"A descendant of yours will always be king;
    I will preserve your dynasty for ever."'

⁵The heavens sing of the wonderful things
    you do;

'... your faithfulness is as permanent as the sky.' (Psalm 89.2)

the holy ones sing of your faithfulness,
    LORD.
⁶No one in heaven is like you, LORD;
    none of the heavenly beings is your equal.
⁷You are feared in the council of the holy ones;
    and all of them stand in awe of you.

⁸LORD God Almighty, none is as mighty as you;
    in all things you are faithful, O LORD.
⁹You rule over the powerful sea;
    you calm its angry waves.

Your kingdom is founded on righteousness and justice.

---

¹⁰You crushed the monster Rahab and killed it;
    with your mighty strength you defeated
    your enemies.
¹¹Heaven is yours, the earth also;
    you made the world and everything in it.
¹²You created the north and the south;
    Mount Tabor and Mount Hermon sing to
    you for joy.
¹³How powerful you are!
    How great is your strength!
¹⁴Your kingdom is founded on righteousness
    and justice;
    love and faithfulness are shown in all you
    do.

¹⁵How happy are the people who worship you
    with songs,
    who live in the light of your kindness!
¹⁶Because of you they rejoice all day long,
    and they praise you for your goodness.
¹⁷You give us great victories;
    in your love you make us triumphant.
¹⁸You, O LORD, chose our protector;
    you, the Holy God of Israel, gave us our
    king.

God's Promise to David

¹⁹In a vision long ago you said to your faithful
    servants,
    'I have given help to a famous soldier;
    I have given the throne to one I chose
    from the people.
²⁰I have made my servant David king
    by anointing him with holy oil.

²¹My strength will always be with him,
    my power will make him strong.
²²His enemies will never succeed against him;
    the wicked will not defeat him.
²³I will crush his foes
    and kill everyone who hates him.
²⁴I will love him and be loyal to him;
    I will make him always victorious.
²⁵I will extend his kingdom
    from the Mediterranean to the River
    Euphrates.
²⁶He will say to me,
    "You are my father and my God;
    you are my protector and saviour."
²⁷I will make him my first-born son,
    the greatest of all kings.
²⁸I will always keep my promise to him,
    and my covenant with him will last for
    ever.
²⁹His dynasty will be as permanent as the sky;
    a descendant of his will always be king.

³⁰'But if his descendants disobey my law
    and do not live according to my
    commands,
³¹if they disregard my instructions
    and do not keep my commandments,

"You are my father and my God."

---

³²then I will punish them for their sins;
    I will make them suffer for their wrongs.
³³But I will not stop loving David
    or fail to keep my promise to him.
³⁴I will not break my covenant with him
    or take back even one promise I made him.

³⁵'Once and for all I have promised by my holy
    name:
    I will never lie to David.
³⁶He will always have descendants,
    and I will watch over his kingdom as long
    as the sun shines.
³⁷It will be as permanent as the moon,
    that faithful witness in the sky.'

Lament over the Defeat of the King

³⁸But you are angry with your chosen king;
    you have deserted and rejected him.

³⁹You have broken your covenant with your
servant
and thrown his crown in the mud.
⁴⁰You have torn down the walls of his city
and left his forts in ruins.
⁴¹All who pass by steal his belongings;
all his neighbours laugh at him.
⁴²You have given the victory to his enemies;
you have made them all happy.
⁴³You have made his weapons useless
and let him be defeated in battle.
⁴⁴You have taken away his royal sceptre
and hurled his throne to the ground.
⁴⁵You have made him old before his time
and covered him with disgrace.

A Prayer for Deliverance

⁴⁶LORD, will you hide yourself for ever?
How long will your anger burn like fire?
⁴⁷Remember how short my life is;

remember that you created all of us
mortal!
⁴⁸Who can live and never die?
How can man keep himself from the
grave?

⁴⁹Lord, where are the former proofs of your
love?
Where are the promises you made to
David?
⁵⁰Don't forget how I, your servant, am
insulted,
how I endure all the curses of the heathen.
⁵¹Your enemies insult your chosen king, O
LORD!
They insult him wherever he goes.

⁵²Praise the LORD for ever!

Amen! Amen!

'How long will your anger burn like fire?' (Psalm 89.46)

BOOK FOUR
(Psalms 90—106)

Of God and Man

90
O Lord, you have always been our home.
[2]Before you created the hills
or brought the world into being,
you were eternally God,
and will be God for ever.

[3]You tell man to return to what he was;
you change him back to dust.
[4]A thousand years to you are like one day;
they are like yesterday, already gone,
like a short hour in the night.
[5]You carry us away like a flood;
we last no longer than a dream.
We are like weeds that sprout in the
morning,
[6] that grow and burst into bloom,
then dry up and die in the evening.

[7]We are destroyed by your anger;
we are terrified by your fury.

**O Lord, you have
always been our home.**

---

[8]You place our sins before you,
our secret sins where you can see them.

[9]Our life is cut short by your anger;
it fades away like a whisper.
[10]Seventy years is all we have—
eighty years, if we are strong;
yet all they bring us is trouble and sorrow;
life is soon over, and we are gone.

[11]Who has felt the full power of your anger?
Who knows what fear your fury can
bring?
[12]Teach us how short our life is,
so that we may become wise.

[13]How much longer will your anger last?
Have pity, O LORD, on your servants!
[14]Fill us each morning with your constant love,
so that we may sing and be glad all our life.
[15]Give us now as much happiness as the
sadness you gave us
during all our years of misery.
[16]Let us, your servants, see your mighty deeds;
let our descendants see your glorious
might.
[17]LORD our God, may your blessings be with us.
Give us success in all we do!

God Our Protector

91
Whoever goes to the LORD for safety,
whoever remains under the
protection of the Almighty,
[2]can say to him,
'You are my defender and protector.
You are my God; in you I trust.'
[3]He will keep you safe from all hidden
dangers
and from all deadly diseases.
[4]He will cover you with his wings;
you will be safe in his care;
his faithfulness will protect and defend
you.
[5]You need not fear any dangers at night
or sudden attacks during the day
[6] or the plagues that strike in the dark
or the evils that kill in daylight.

[7]A thousand may fall dead beside you,
ten thousand all round you,
but you will not be harmed.
[8]You will look and see
how the wicked are punished.

[9]You have made the LORD your defender,
the Most High your protector,

**He will cover you
with his wings;
you will be safe in his care.**

---

[10]and so no disaster will strike you,
no violence will come near your home.
[11]God will put his angels in charge of you
to protect you wherever you go.
[12]They will hold you up with their hands

to keep you from hurting your feet on the
stones.
¹³You will trample down lions and snakes,
fierce lions and poisonous snakes.

¹⁴God says, 'I will save those who love me
and will protect those who acknowledge
me as LORD.
¹⁵When they call to me, I will answer them;
when they are in trouble, I will be with
them.
I will rescue them and honour them.
¹⁶I will reward them with long life;
I will save them.'

A Song of Praise

92 How good it is to give thanks to
you, O LORD,
to sing in your honour, O Most
High God,
²to proclaim your constant love every
morning
and your faithfulness every night,
³with the music of stringed instruments
and with melody on the harp.
⁴Your mighty deeds, O LORD, make me glad;
because of what you have done, I sing for
joy.

⁵How great are your actions, LORD!

How deep are your thoughts!
⁶This is something a fool cannot know;
a stupid man cannot understand:
⁷the wicked may grow like weeds,
those who do wrong may prosper;
yet they will be totally destroyed,
⁸ because you, LORD, are supreme for ever.

⁹We know that your enemies will die,
and all the wicked will be defeated.
¹⁰You have made me as strong as a wild ox;
you have blessed me with happiness.
¹¹I have seen the defeat of my enemies
and heard the cries of the wicked.

¹²The righteous will flourish like palm-trees;
they will grow like the cedars of Lebanon.
¹³They are like trees planted in the house of
the LORD,
that flourish in the Temple of our God,
¹⁴ that still bear fruit in old age
and are always green and strong.

**They are like trees ...
that still bear fruit in old age
and are always green and strong.**

---

¹⁵This shows that the LORD is just,
that there is no wrong in my protector.

'The righteous ... will grow like the cedars of Lebanon.' (Psalm 92.12)

God the King

93 The LORD is king.
He is clothed with majesty and
strength.
The earth is set firmly in place
and cannot be moved.
²Your throne, O LORD, has been firm from the
beginning,
and you existed before time began.

³The ocean depths raise their voice, O LORD;
they raise their voice and roar.
⁴The LORD rules supreme in heaven,
greater than the roar of the ocean,
more powerful than the waves of the sea.

⁵Your laws are eternal, LORD,
and your Temple is holy indeed,
for ever and ever.

God the Judge of All

94 LORD, you are a God who
punishes;
reveal your anger!
²You are the judge of all men;
rise and give the proud what they deserve!
³How much longer will the wicked be glad?
How much longer, LORD?
⁴How much longer will criminals be proud
and boast about their crimes?

⁵They crush your people, LORD;
they oppress those who belong to you.
⁶They kill widows and orphans,
and murder the strangers who live in our
land.
⁷They say, 'The LORD does not see us;
the God of Israel does not notice.'

⁸My people, how can you be such stupid fools?
When will you ever learn?

My people ... When will you ever learn?

---

⁹God made our ears—can't he hear?
He made our eyes—can't he see?
¹⁰He scolds the nations—won't he punish
them?

He is the teacher of all men—hasn't he
any knowledge?
¹¹The LORD knows what they think;
he knows how senseless their reasoning
is.

¹²LORD, how happy is the person you instruct,
the one to whom you teach your law!
¹³You give him rest from days of trouble
until a pit is dug to trap the wicked.

The LORD will not abandon his people.

---

¹⁴The LORD will not abandon his people;
he will not desert those who belong to
him.
¹⁵Justice will again be found in the courts,
and all righteous people will support it.

¹⁶Who stood up for me against the wicked?
Who took my side against the evildoers?
¹⁷If the LORD had not helped me,
I would have gone quickly to the land of
silence.
¹⁸I said, 'I am falling';
but your constant love, O LORD, held me
up.
¹⁹Whenever I am anxious and worried,
you comfort me and make me glad.

²⁰You have nothing to do with corrupt judges,
who make injustice legal,
²¹ who plot against good men
and sentence the innocent to death.
²²But the LORD defends me;
my God protects me.
²³He will punish them for their wickedness
and destroy them for their sins;
the LORD our God will destroy them.

A Song of Praise

95 Come, let us praise the LORD!
Let us sing for joy to God, who
protects us!
²Let us come before him with thanksgiving
and sing joyful songs of praise.
³For the LORD is a mighty God,
a mighty king over all the gods.

⁴He rules over the whole earth,
    from the deepest caves to the highest hills.
⁵He rules over the sea, which he made;
    the land also, which he himself formed.

⁶Come, let us bow down and worship him;
    let us kneel before the LORD, our Maker!

**He is our God;
we are the people he cares for,
the flock for which he provides.**

⁷He is our God;
    we are the people he cares for,
    the flock for which he provides.

Listen today to what he says:
⁸'Don't be stubborn, as your ancestors were
        at Meribah,
    as they were that day in the desert at
        Massah.
⁹There they put me to the test and tried me,
    although they had seen what I did for
        them.
¹⁰For forty years I was disgusted with those
        people.
    I said, "How disloyal they are!
    They refuse to obey my commands."
¹¹I was angry and made a solemn promise:
    "You will never enter the land
    where I would have given you rest."'

God the Supreme King

96
Sing a new song to the LORD!
    Sing to the LORD, all the world!
²Sing to the LORD, and praise him!
Proclaim every day the good news that he
    has saved us.
³Proclaim his glory to the nations,
    his mighty deeds to all peoples.

⁴The LORD is great and is to be highly praised;
    he is to be honoured more than all the
        gods.
⁵The gods of all other nations are only idols,
    but the LORD created the heavens.
⁶Glory and majesty surround him;
    power and beauty fill his Temple.

⁷Praise the LORD, all people on earth;
    praise his glory and might.
⁸Praise the LORD's glorious name;
    bring an offering and come into his
        Temple.
⁹Bow down before the Holy One when he
        appears;
    tremble before him, all the earth!

¹⁰Say to all the nations, 'The LORD is king!
    The earth is set firmly in place and cannot
        be moved;
    he will judge the peoples with justice.'
¹¹Be glad, earth and sky!
    Roar, sea, and every creature in you;
¹²   be glad, fields, and everything in you!
The trees in the woods will shout for joy
¹³   when the LORD comes to rule the earth.
He will rule the peoples of the world
    with justice and fairness.

'Be glad, earth and sky!' (Psalm 96.11)

God the Supreme Ruler

97

The LORD is king! Earth, be glad!
Rejoice, you islands of the seas!
[2]Clouds and darkness surround
him;
he rules with righteousness and justice.
[3]Fire goes in front of him
and burns up his enemies round him.
[4]His lightning lights up the world;
the earth sees it and trembles.
[5]The hills melt like wax before the LORD,
before the Lord of all the earth.

**The LORD loves those
who hate evil;
he protects
the lives of his people.**

---

[6]The heavens proclaim his righteousness,
and all the nations see his glory.

[7]Everyone who worships idols is put to
shame;
all the gods bow down before the LORD.
[8]The people of Zion are glad,
and the cities of Judah rejoice
because of your judgements, O LORD.
[9]LORD Almighty, you are ruler of all the earth;
you are much greater than all the gods.

[10]The LORD loves those who hate evil;
he protects the lives of his people;
he rescues them from the power of the
wicked.
[11]Light shines on the righteous,
and gladness on the good.
[12]All you that are righteous be glad
because of what the LORD has done!
Remember what the holy God has done,
and give thanks to him.

God the Ruler of the World

98

Sing a new song to the LORD;
he has done wonderful things!
By his own power and holy
strength
he has won the victory.
[2]The LORD announced his victory;

he made his saving power known to the
nations.
[3]He kept his promise to the people of Israel
with loyalty and constant love for them.
All people everywhere have seen the victory
of our God.

[4]Sing for joy to the LORD, all the earth;
praise him with songs and shouts of joy!
[5]Sing praises to the LORD!
Play music on the harps!
[6]Blow trumpets and horns,
and shout for joy to the LORD, our king.

[7]Roar, sea, and every creature in you;
sing, earth, and all who live on you!
[8]Clap your hands, you rivers;
you hills, sing together with joy before the
LORD,
[9]   because he comes to rule the earth.
He will rule the peoples of the world
with justice and fairness.

God the Supreme King

99

The LORD is king;
and the people tremble.
He is enthroned above the
winged creatures
and the earth shakes.
[2]The LORD is mighty in Zion;
he is supreme over all the nations.
[3]Everyone will praise his great and majestic
name.
Holy is he!

[4]Mighty king, you love what is right;
you have established justice in Israel;
you have brought righteousness and
fairness.
[5]Praise the LORD our God;
worship before his throne!
Holy is he!

[6]Moses and Aaron were his priests,
and Samuel was one who prayed to him;
they called to the LORD, and he answered
them.
[7]He spoke to them from the pillar of cloud;
they obeyed the laws and commands that
he gave them.

'Sing for joy to the LORD, all the earth.' (Psalm 98.4)

⁸O LORD, our God, you answered your people;
    you showed them that you are a God who
        forgives,
    even though you punished them for their
        sins.
⁹Praise the LORD our God,
    and worship at his sacred hill!
The LORD our God is holy.

A Hymn of Praise

100
Sing to the LORD, all the
        world!
²Worship the LORD with joy;
    come before him with happy songs!

³Acknowledge that the LORD is God.
    He made us, and we belong to him;
    we are his people, we are his flock.

Sing to the LORD, all the world!

⁴Enter the temple gates with thanksgiving,
    go into its courts with praise.
    Give thanks to him and praise him.

⁵The LORD is good;
    his love is eternal
    and his faithfulness lasts for ever.

A King's Promise

101
My song is about loyalty and
        justice,
    and I sing it to you, O LORD.
²My conduct will be faultless.
    When will you come to me?

I will live a pure life in my house,
³   and will never tolerate evil.
I hate the actions of those who turn away
        from God;
    I will have nothing to do with them.
⁴I will not be dishonest,
    and will have no dealings with evil.
⁵I will get rid of anyone
    who whispers evil things about someone
        else;
I will not tolerate a man
    who is proud and arrogant.

⁶I will approve of those who are faithful to
    God

and will let them live in my palace.
Those who are completely honest
will be allowed to serve me.

[7]No liar will live in my palace;
no hypocrite will remain in my presence.
[8]Day after day I will destroy
the wicked in our land;
I will expel all evil men
from the city of the LORD.

The Prayer of a Troubled Young Man

102

Listen to my prayer, O LORD,
and hear my cry for help!
[2]When I am in trouble,
don't turn away from me!
Listen to me,
and answer me quickly when I call!

[3]My life is disappearing like smoke;
my body is burning like fire.
[4]I am beaten down like dry grass;
I have lost my desire for food.
[5]I groan aloud;
I am nothing but skin and bones.
[6]I am like a wild bird in the desert,
like an owl in abandoned ruins.
[7]I lie awake;
I am like a lonely bird on a house-top.
[8]All day long my enemies insult me;
those who mock me use my name in
cursing.

[9-10]Because of your anger and fury,
ashes are my food,
and my tears are mixed with my drink.
You picked me up and threw me away.
[11]My life is like the evening shadows;
I am like dry grass.

[12]But you, O LORD, are king for ever;
all generations will remember you.
[13]You will rise and take pity on Zion;
the time has come to have mercy on
her;
this is the right time.
[14]Your servants love her,
even though she is destroyed;
they have pity on her,
even though she is in ruins.

[15]The nations will fear the LORD;
all the kings of the earth will fear his
power.
[16]When the LORD rebuilds Zion,
he will reveal his greatness.
[17]He will hear his forsaken people
and listen to their prayer.

[18]Write down for the coming generation what
the LORD has done,
so that people not yet born will praise him.
[19]The LORD looked down from his holy place
on high,
he looked down from heaven to earth.
[20]He heard the groans of prisoners
and set free those who were condemned
to die.
[21]And so his name will be proclaimed in Zion,
and he will be praised in Jerusalem
[22]   when nations and kingdoms come
together
and worship the LORD.

[23]The LORD has made me weak while I am still
young;
he has shortened my life.
[24]O God, do not take me away now
before I grow old.

O LORD, you live for ever;
[25]   long ago you created the earth,
and with your own hands you made the
heavens.

**O LORD, you live for ever;
long ago
you created the earth,
and with your own hands
you made the heavens.**

---

[26]They will disappear, but you will remain;
they will all wear out like clothes.
You will discard them like clothes,
and they will vanish.
[27]But you are always the same,
and your life never ends.
[28]Our children will live in safety,
and under your protection
their descendants will be secure.

The Love of God

103 Praise the LORD, my soul!
All my being, praise his
holy name!

²Praise the LORD, my soul,
and do not forget how kind he is.
³He forgives all my sins
and heals all my diseases.
⁴He keeps me from the grave
and blesses me with love and mercy.
⁵He fills my life with good things,
so that I stay young and strong like an
eagle.

**He fills my life
with good things,
so that I stay young
and strong like an eagle.**

---

⁶The LORD judges in favour of the oppressed
and gives them their rights.
⁷He revealed his plans to Moses
and let the people of Israel see his mighty
deeds.
⁸The LORD is merciful and loving,
slow to become angry and full of constant
love.
⁹He does not keep on rebuking;
he is not angry for ever.
¹⁰He does not punish us as we deserve
or repay us according to our sins and
wrongs.
¹¹As high as the sky is above the earth,
so great is his love for those who honour
him.
¹²As far as the east is from the west,
so far does he remove our sins from us.
¹³As a father is kind to his children,
so the LORD is kind to those who honour
him.
¹⁴He knows what we are made of;
he remembers that we are dust.

¹⁵As for us, our life is like grass.
We grow and flourish like a wild flower;
¹⁶ then the wind blows on it, and it is gone—
no one sees it again.
¹⁷But for those who honour the LORD, his love
lasts for ever,

and his goodness endures for all
generations
¹⁸of those who are true to his covenant
and who faithfully obey his commands.

¹⁹The LORD placed his throne in heaven;
he is king over all.
²⁰Praise the LORD, you strong and mighty
angels,
who obey his commands,
who listen to what he says.
²¹Praise the LORD, all you heavenly powers,
you servants of his, who do his will!
²²Praise the LORD, all his creatures
in all the places he rules.
Praise the LORD, my soul!

In Praise of the Creator

104 Praise the LORD, my soul!
O LORD, my God, how
great you are!

You are clothed with majesty and glory;
²   you cover yourself with light.
You have spread out the heavens like a tent
³   and built your home on the waters above.
You use the clouds as your chariot
and ride on the wings of the wind.
⁴You use the winds as your messengers
and flashes of lightning as your servants.

'We grow and flourish like a wild flower.' (Psalm 103.15)

⁵You have set the earth firmly on its
      foundations,
   and it will never be moved.
⁶You placed the ocean over it like a robe,
   and the water covered the mountains.
⁷When you rebuked the waters, they fled;
   they rushed away when they heard your
      shout of command.
⁸They flowed over the mountains and into
      the valleys,
   to the place you had made for them.
⁹You set a boundary they can never pass,
   to keep them from covering the earth
      again.

¹⁰You make springs flow in the valleys,
   and rivers run between the hills.
¹¹They provide water for the wild animals;
   there the wild donkeys quench their thirst.
¹²In the trees near by,
   the birds make their nests and sing.

¹³From the sky you send rain on the hills,
   and the earth is filled with your blessings.

**LORD, you have made
so many things!
How wisely you made them all!**

---

¹⁴You make grass grow for the cattle
   and plants for man to use,
   so that he can grow his crops
¹⁵   and produce wine to make him happy,
   olive-oil to make him cheerful,
   and bread to give him strength.

¹⁶The cedars of Lebanon get plenty of rain—
   the LORD's own trees, which he planted.
¹⁷There the birds build their nests;
   the storks nest in the fir-trees.
¹⁸The wild goats live in the high mountains,
   and the rock-badgers hide in the cliffs.

¹⁹You created the moon to mark the months;
   the sun knows the time to set.
²⁰You made the night, and in the darkness
   all the wild animals come out.
²¹The young lions roar while they hunt,
   looking for the food that God provides.

²²When the sun rises, they go back
   and lie down in their dens.
²³Then people go out to do their work
   and keep working until evening.

²⁴LORD, you have made so many things!
   How wisely you made them all!
   The earth is filled with your creatures.
²⁵There is the ocean, large and wide,
   where countless creatures live,
   large and small alike.
²⁶The ships sail on it, and in it plays Leviathan,
   that sea-monster which you made.

²⁷All of them depend on you
   to give them food when they need it.
²⁸You give it to them, and they eat it;
   you provide food, and they are satisfied.
²⁹When you turn away, they are afraid;
   when you take away your breath, they die
   and go back to the dust from which they
      came.
³⁰But when you give them breath, they are
      created;
   you give new life to the earth.

³¹May the glory of the LORD last for ever!
   May the LORD be happy with what he has
      made!
³²He looks at the earth, and it trembles;
   he touches the mountains, and they pour
      out smoke.

³³I will sing to the LORD all my life;
   as long as I live I will sing praises to my
      God.
³⁴May he be pleased with my song,
   for my gladness comes from him.
³⁵May sinners be destroyed from the earth;
   may the wicked be no more.

Praise the LORD, my soul!
Praise the LORD!

God and His People

105

Give thanks to the LORD,
   proclaim his greatness;
   tell the nations what he has
      done.
²Sing praise to the LORD;

'The earth is filled with your creatures.' (Psalm104.24)

tell of the wonderful things he has done.
³Be glad that we belong to him;
  let all who worship him rejoice.
⁴Go to the LORD for help;
  and worship him continually.
⁵⁻⁶You descendants of Abraham, his servant;
  you descendants of Jacob, the man he
    chose:
remember the miracles that God performed
  and the judgements that he gave.

⁷The LORD is our God;
  his commands are for all the world.

Go to the LORD for help.

---

⁸He will keep his covenant for ever,
  his promises for a thousand generations.
⁹He will keep the agreement he made with
    Abraham
  and his promise to Isaac.
¹⁰The LORD made a covenant with Jacob,
  one that will last for ever.
¹¹'I will give you the land of Canaan,' he said.
  'It will be your own possession.'

¹²God's people were few in number,
  strangers in the land of Canaan.
¹³They wandered from country to country,
  from one kingdom to another.
¹⁴But God let no one oppress them;
  to protect them, he warned the kings:
¹⁵'Don't harm my chosen servants;
  do not touch my prophets.'

¹⁶The LORD sent famine to their country
  and took away all their food.
¹⁷But he sent a man ahead of them,
  Joseph, who had been sold as a slave.
¹⁸His feet were kept in chains,
  and an iron collar was round his neck,
¹⁹ until what he had predicted came true.
The word of the LORD proved him right.
²⁰Then the king of Egypt had him released;
  the ruler of nations set him free.
²¹He put him in charge of his government
  and made him ruler over all the land,
²² with power over the king's officials
  and authority to instruct his advisers.

²³Then Jacob went to Egypt
  and settled in that country.
²⁴The LORD gave many children to his people
  and made them stronger than their
    enemies.
²⁵He made the Egyptians hate his people
  and treat his servants with deceit.

²⁶Then he sent his servant Moses,
  and Aaron, whom he had chosen.
²⁷They did God's mighty acts
  and performed miracles in Egypt.
²⁸God sent darkness on the country,
  but the Egyptians did not obey his
    command.
²⁹He turned their rivers into blood
  and killed all their fish.
³⁰Their country was overrun with frogs,
  even the palace was filled with them.
³¹God commanded, and flies and gnats
  swarmed throughout the whole country.
³²He sent hail and lightning on their land
  instead of rain;
³³he destroyed their grapevines and fig-trees
  and broke down all the trees.
³⁴He commanded, and the locusts came,
  countless millions of them;

So he led his chosen people out,
and they sang
and shouted for joy.

---

³⁵they ate all the plants in the land;
  they ate all the crops.
³⁶He killed the first-born sons
  of all the families of Egypt.

³⁷Then he led the Israelites out;
  they carried silver and gold,
  and all of them were healthy and strong.
³⁸The Egyptians were afraid of them
  and were glad when they left.
³⁹God put a cloud over his people
  and a fire at night to give them light.
⁴⁰They asked, and he sent quails;
  he gave them food from heaven to satisfy
    them.
⁴¹He opened a rock, and water gushed out,
  flowing through the desert like a river.

⁴²He remembered his sacred promise
　　to Abraham his servant.

⁴³So he led his chosen people out,
　　and they sang and shouted for joy.
⁴⁴He gave them the lands of other peoples
　　and let them take over their fields,
⁴⁵so that his people would obey his laws
　　and keep all his commands.

Praise the LORD!

The LORD's Goodness to His People

106

Praise the LORD!

Give thanks to the LORD,
　　　　because he is good;
　his love is eternal.
²Who can tell all the great things he has done?
　Who can praise him enough?
³Happy are those who obey his commands,
　who always do what is right.

⁴Remember me, LORD, when you help your
　　　　people;
　include me when you save them.
⁵Let me see the prosperity of your people
　　and share in the happiness of your nation,
　　in the glad pride of those who belong to
　　you.

⁶We have sinned as our ancestors did;
　we have been wicked and evil.
⁷Our ancestors in Egypt did not understand
　　God's wonderful acts;
　they forgot the many times he showed
　　them his love,
　and they rebelled against the Almighty at
　　the Red Sea.

He rescued them from their enemies.

---

⁸But he saved them, as he had promised,
　　in order to show his great power.
⁹He gave a command to the Red Sea,
　　and it dried up;
　he led his people across on dry land.
¹⁰He saved them from those who hated them;

he rescued them from their enemies.
¹¹But the water drowned their enemies;
　not one of them was left.
¹²Then his people believed his promises
　　and sang praises to him.

¹³But they quickly forgot what he had done
　　and acted without waiting for his advice.
¹⁴They were filled with craving in the desert
　　and put God to the test;
¹⁵so he gave them what they asked for,
　　but also sent a terrible disease among
　　them.

¹⁶There in the desert they were jealous of
　　Moses
　and of Aaron, the LORD's holy servant.
¹⁷Then the earth opened up and swallowed
　　Dathan
　and buried Abiram and his family;
¹⁸fire came down on their followers
　　and burnt up those wicked people.

'Remember me, LORD, when you help your people.' (Psalm 106.4)

¹⁹They made a gold bull-calf at Sinai
    and worshipped that idol;
²⁰they exchanged the glory of God
    for the image of an animal that eats grass.
²¹They forgot the God who had saved them
    by his mighty acts in Egypt.

**They forgot the God
who had saved them
by his mighty acts in Egypt.**

---

²²What wonderful things he did there!
    What amazing things at the Red Sea!
²³When God said that he would destroy his
        people,
    his chosen servant, Moses, stood up
        against God
    and prevented his anger from destroying
        them.

²⁴Then they rejected the pleasant land,
    because they did not believe God's
        promise.
²⁵They stayed in their tents and grumbled
    and would not listen to the LORD.
²⁶So he gave them a solemn warning
    that he would make them die in the desert
²⁷   and scatter their descendants among the
        heathen,
    letting them die in foreign countries.

²⁸Then at Peor, God's people joined in the
        worship of Baal,
    and ate sacrifices offered to lifeless gods.
²⁹They stirred up the LORD's anger by their
        actions,
    and a terrible disease broke out among
        them.
³⁰But Phinehas stood up and punished the
        guilty,
    and the plague was stopped.
³¹This has been remembered in his favour
        ever since
    and will be for all time to come.

³²At the springs of Meribah the people made
        the LORD angry,
    and Moses was in trouble on their account.
³³They made him so bitter

that he spoke without stopping to think.

³⁴They did not kill the heathen,
    as the LORD had commanded them to do,
³⁵but they intermarried with them
    and adopted their pagan ways.
³⁶God's people worshipped idols,
    and this caused their destruction.
³⁷They offered their own sons and daughters
    as sacrifices to the idols of Canaan.
³⁸They killed those innocent children,
    and the land was defiled by those
        murders.
³⁹They made themselves impure by their
        actions
    and were unfaithful to God.

⁴⁰So the LORD was angry with his people;
    he was disgusted with them.
⁴¹He abandoned them to the power of the
        heathen,
    and their enemies ruled over them.
⁴²They were oppressed by their enemies
    and were in complete subjection to them.
⁴³Many times the LORD rescued his people,
    but they chose to rebel against him
    and sank deeper into sin.
⁴⁴Yet the LORD heard them when they cried out,
    and he took notice of their distress.

**Many times the LORD
rescued his people ...**

---

⁴⁵For their sake he remembered his covenant,
    and because of his great love he relented.
⁴⁶He made all their oppressors
    feel sorry for them.

⁴⁷Save us, O LORD our God,
    and bring us back from among the
        nations,
    so that we may be thankful
    and praise your holy name.

⁴⁸Praise the LORD, the God of Israel;
    praise him now and for ever!
    Let everyone say, 'Amen!'

Praise the LORD!

BOOK FIVE
(Psalms 107–150)

In Praise of God's Goodness

107
¹'Give thanks to the LORD,
because he is good;
his love is eternal!'
²Repeat these words in praise to the LORD,
all you whom he has saved.
He has rescued you from your enemies
³ and has brought you back from foreign
countries,
from east and west, from north and south.

⁴Some wandered in the trackless desert
and could not find their way to a city to
live in.
⁵They were hungry and thirsty
and had given up all hope.
⁶Then in their trouble they called to the LORD,
and he saved them from their distress.
⁷He led them by a straight road
to a city where they could live.
⁸They must thank the LORD for his constant
love,
for the wonderful things he did for them.
⁹He satisfies those who are thirsty
and fills the hungry with good things.

¹⁰Some were living in gloom and darkness,
prisoners suffering in chains,
¹¹because they had rebelled against the
commands of Almighty God
and had rejected his instructions.
¹²They were worn out from hard work;
they would fall down, and no one would
help.
¹³Then in their trouble they called to the LORD,
and he saved them from their distress.
¹⁴He brought them out of their gloom and
darkness
and broke their chains in pieces.

**'Give thanks to the LORD,
because he is good; his love is eternal!'**

---

¹⁵They must thank the LORD for his constant
love,
for the wonderful things he did for them.
¹⁶He breaks down doors of bronze
and smashes iron bars.

¹⁷Some were fools, suffering because of their
sins
and because of their evil;
¹⁸they couldn't stand the sight of food
and were close to death.
¹⁹Then in their trouble they called to the LORD,
and he saved them from their distress.

'He brought them out of their gloom and darkness and broke their chains in pieces.' (Psalm 107.14)

²⁰He healed them with his command
and saved them from the grave.
²¹They must thank the LORD for his constant
love,
for the wonderful things he did for them.
²²They must thank him with sacrifices,
and with songs of joy must tell all that he
has done.

²³Some sailed over the ocean in ships,
earning their living on the seas.

**He changed deserts
into pools of water
and dry land into flowing springs.**

---

²⁴They saw what the LORD can do,
his wonderful acts on the seas.
²⁵He commanded, and a mighty wind began to
blow
and stirred up the waves.
²⁶The ships were lifted high in the air
and plunged down into the depths.
In such danger the men lost their courage;
²⁷   they stumbled and staggered like
drunken men—
all their skill was useless.
²⁸Then in their trouble they called to the LORD,
and he saved them from their distress.
²⁹He calmed the raging storm,
and the waves became quiet.
³⁰They were glad because of the calm,
and he brought them safe to the port they
wanted.
³¹They must thank the LORD for his constant
love,
for the wonderful things he did for them.
³²They must proclaim his greatness in the
assembly of the people
and praise him before the council of the
leaders.

³³The LORD made rivers dry up completely
and stopped springs from flowing.
³⁴He made rich soil become a salty wilderness
because of the wickedness of those who
lived there.
³⁵He changed deserts into pools of water
and dry land into flowing springs.

³⁶He let hungry people settle there,
and they built a city to live in.
³⁷They sowed the fields and planted
grapevines
and reaped an abundant harvest.
³⁸He blessed his people, and they had many
children;
he kept their herds of cattle from
decreasing.

³⁹When God's people were defeated and
humiliated
by cruel oppression and suffering,
⁴⁰he showed contempt for their oppressors
and made them wander in trackless
deserts.
⁴¹But he rescued the needy from their misery
and made their families increase like
flocks.
⁴²The righteous see this and are glad,
but all the wicked are put to silence.

⁴³May those who are wise think about these
things;
may they consider the LORD's constant
love.

A Prayer for Help against Enemies

108

I have complete confidence, O
God!
I will sing and praise you!
Wake up, my soul!
²   Wake up, my harp and lyre!
I will wake up the sun.
³I will thank you, O LORD, among the nations.
I will praise you among the peoples.
⁴Your constant love reaches above the
heavens;
your faithfulness touches the skies.

⁵Show your greatness in the sky, O God,
and your glory over all the earth.
⁶Save us by your might; answer my prayer,
so that the people you love may be
rescued.

⁷From his sanctuary God has said,
'In triumph I will divide Shechem
and distribute the Valley of Sukkoth to my
people.

[8]Gilead is mine, and Manasseh too;
    Ephraim is my helmet
    and Judah my royal sceptre.
[9]But I will use Moab as my wash-basin
    and I will throw my sandals on Edom,
        as a sign that I own it.
    I will shout in triumph over the
        Philistines.'

[10]Who, O God, will take me into the fortified
        city?
    Who will lead me to Edom?
[11]Have you really rejected us?
    Aren't you going to march out with our
        armies?

Human help is worthless.

---

[12]Help us against the enemy;
    human help is worthless.
[13]With God on our side we will win;
    he will defeat our enemies.

The Complaint of a Man in Trouble

109

[1]I praise you, God; don't
        remain silent!
[2]Wicked men and liars have
        attacked me.
They tell lies about me
[3]   and they say evil things about me, •
    attacking me for no reason.
[4]They oppose me, even though I love them
    and have prayed for them.
[5]They pay me back evil for good
    and hatred for love.

[6]Choose some corrupt judge to try my enemy,
    and let one of his own enemies accuse him.
[7]May he be tried and found guilty;
    may even his prayer be considered a
        crime!
[8]May his life soon be ended;
    may another man take his job!
[9]May his children become orphans,
    and his wife a widow!
[10]May his children be homeless beggars;
    may they be driven from the ruins they
        live in!

[11]May his creditors take away all his property,
    and may strangers get everything he
        worked for.
[12]May no one ever be kind to him
    or care for the orphans he leaves behind.
[13]May all his descendants die,
    and may his name be forgotten in the next
        generation.
[14]May the LORD remember the evil of his
        ancestors
    and never forgive his mother's sins.
[15]May the LORD always remember their sins,
    but may they themselves be completely
        forgotten!

[16]That man never thought of being kind;
    he persecuted and killed
    the poor, the needy, and the helpless.
[17]He loved to curse—may he be cursed!
    He hated to give blessings—may no one
        bless him!
[18]He cursed as naturally as he dressed himself;
    may his own curses soak into his body like
        water
    and into his bones like oil!
[19]May they cover him like clothes
    and always be round him like a belt!

[20]LORD, punish my enemies in that way—
    those who say such evil things against me!
[21]But my Sovereign LORD, help me as you have
        promised,
    and rescue me because of the goodness of
        your love.

'... help me as you have promised ...' (Psalm 109.21)

²²I am poor and needy;
   I am hurt to the depths of my heart.
²³Like an evening shadow I am about to vanish;
   I am blown away like an insect.
²⁴My knees are weak from lack of food;
   I am nothing but skin and bones.
²⁵When people see me, they laugh at me;
   they shake their heads in scorn.

²⁶Help me, O LORD my God;
   because of your constant love, save me!
²⁷Make my enemies know
   that you are the one who saves me.
²⁸They may curse me, but you will bless me.
   May my persecutors be defeated,
   and may I, your servant, be glad.

**Make my enemies know
that you are the one who saves me.**

===

²⁹May my enemies be covered with disgrace;
   may they wear their shame like a robe.

³⁰I will give loud thanks to the LORD;
   I will praise him in the assembly of the
   people,
³¹because he defends the poor man
   and saves him from those who condemn
   him to death.

The LORD and His Chosen King

110

The LORD said to my lord, the king,
   'Sit here at my right
until I put your enemies under your feet.'
²From Zion the LORD will extend your royal
   power.
   'Rule over your enemies,' he says.
³On the day you fight your enemies,
   your people will volunteer.
Like the dew of early morning
   your young men will come to you on the
   sacred hills.

⁴The LORD made a solemn promise and will
   not take it back:
   'You will be a priest for ever
   in the priestly order of Melchizedek.'

⁵The Lord is at your right side;
   when he becomes angry, he will defeat
   kings.
⁶He will pass judgement on the nations
   and fill the battlefield with corpses;
   he will defeat kings all over the earth.
⁷The king will drink from the stream by the
   road,
   and strengthened, he will stand victorious.

In Praise of the LORD

111

Praise the LORD!

With all my heart I will thank
   the LORD
in the assembly of his people.
²How wonderful are the things the LORD does!
   All who are delighted with them want to
   understand them.
³All he does is full of honour and majesty;
   his righteousness is eternal.

⁴The LORD does not let us forget his
   wonderful actions;
   he is kind and merciful.
⁵He provides food for those who honour him;
   he never forgets his covenant.
⁶He has shown his power to his people
   by giving them the lands of foreigners.

⁷In all he does he is faithful and just;
   all his commands are dependable.
⁸They last for all time;
   they were given in truth and
   righteousness.
⁹He set his people free
   and made an eternal covenant with
   them.

**The way to become wise
is to honour the LORD.**

===

Holy and mighty is he!
¹⁰The way to become wise is to honour the
   LORD;
   he gives sound judgement to all who obey
   his commands.
He is to be praised for ever.

The Happiness of a Good Person

112
Praise the LORD!

Happy is the person who
honours the LORD,
who takes pleasure in obeying his
commands.
²The good man's children will be powerful in
the land;
his descendants will be blessed.
³His family will be wealthy and rich,
and he will be prosperous for ever.

⁴Light shines in the darkness for good men,

¹⁰The wicked see this and are angry;
they glare in hate and disappear;
their hopes are gone for ever.

In Praise of the LORD's Goodness

113
Praise the LORD!

You servants of the LORD,
praise his name!
²May his name be praised,
now and for ever.
³From the east to the west
praise the name of the LORD!

'The good man's ... descendants will be blessed.' (Psalm 112.2)

for those who are merciful, kind, and just.
Happy is the person who is generous with
his loans,
who runs his business honestly.
⁶A good person will never fail;
he will always be remembered.

⁷He is not afraid of receiving bad news;
his faith is strong, and he trusts in the
LORD.
⁸He is not worried or afraid;
he is certain to see his enemies defeated.
⁹He gives generously to the needy,
and his kindness never fails;
he will be powerful and respected.

⁴The LORD rules over all nations;
his glory is above the heavens.

⁵There is no one like the LORD our God.
He lives in the heights above,
⁶   but he bends down
to see the heavens and the earth.
⁷He raises the poor from the dust;
he lifts the needy from their misery
⁸and makes them companions of princes,
the princes of his people.
⁹He honours the childless wife in her home;
he makes her happy by giving her children.

Praise the LORD!

I will sing to the Lord
all my life;
as long as I live I will sing
praises to my God.

Psalm 104.33

A Passover Song

114

When the people of Israel left
Egypt,
when Jacob's descendants
left that foreign land,
[2]Judah became the Lord's holy people,
Israel became his own possession.

[3]The Red Sea looked and ran away;
the River Jordan stopped flowing.
[4]The mountains skipped like goats;
the hills jumped about like lambs.

[5]What happened, Sea, to make you run
away?
And you, O Jordan, why did you stop
flowing?
[6]You mountains, why did you skip like goats?
You hills, why did you jump about like
lambs?

[7]Tremble, earth, at the Lord's coming,
at the presence of the God of Jacob,
[8]who changes rocks into pools of water
and solid cliffs into flowing springs.

The One True God

115

To you alone, O LORD, to you
alone,
and not to us, must glory
be given
because of your constant love and
faithfulness.

[2]Why should the nations ask us,
'Where is your God?'
[3]Our God is in heaven;
he does whatever he wishes.
[4]Their gods are made of silver and gold,
formed by human hands.
[5]They have mouths, but cannot speak,
and eyes, but cannot see.
[6]They have ears, but cannot hear,
and noses, but cannot smell.
[7]They have hands, but cannot feel,
and feet, but cannot walk;
they cannot make a sound.
[8]May all who made them and who trust in
them
become like the idols they have made.

[9]Trust in the LORD, you people of Israel.
He helps you and protects you.
[10]Trust in the LORD, you priests of God.
He helps you and protects you.
[11]Trust in the LORD, all you that worship him.
He helps you and protects you.

[12]The LORD remembers us and will bless us;
he will bless the people of Israel
and all the priests of God.

**Trust in the LORD,
all you that worship him.
He helps you and protects you.**

---

[13]He will bless everyone who honours him,
the great and the small alike.

[14]May the LORD give you children—
you and your descendants!
[15]May you be blessed by the LORD,
who made heaven and earth!

[16]Heaven belongs to the LORD alone,
but he gave the earth to man.
[17]The LORD is not praised by the dead,
by any who go down to the land of silence.
[18]But we, the living, will give thanks to him
now and for ever.

Praise the LORD!

A Man Saved from Death Praises God

116

I love the LORD, because he
hears me;
he listens to my prayers.
[2]He listens to me
every time I call to him.
[3]The danger of death was all round me;
the horrors of the grave closed in on me;
I was filled with fear and anxiety.
[4]Then I called to the LORD,
'I beg you, LORD, save me!'

[5]The LORD is merciful and good;
our God is compassionate.
[6]The LORD protects the helpless;
when I was in danger, he saved me.

⁷Be confident, my heart,
     because the LORD has been good to me.

⁸The LORD saved me from death;
     he stopped my tears
     and kept me from defeat.
⁹And so I walk in the presence of the LORD
     in the world of the living.
¹⁰I kept on believing, even when I said,
     'I am completely crushed,'
¹¹even when I was afraid and said,
     'No one can be trusted.'

What can I offer the LORD?

¹²What can I offer the LORD
     for all his goodness to me?
¹³I will bring a wine-offering to the LORD,
     to thank him for saving me.
¹⁴In the assembly of all his people
     I will give him what I have promised.

¹⁵How painful it is to the LORD
     when one of his people dies!
¹⁶I am your servant, LORD;
     I serve you, just as my mother did.

I am your servant, LORD.

You have saved me from death.
¹⁷I will give you a sacrifice of thanksgiving
     and offer my prayer to you.
¹⁸⁻¹⁹In the assembly of all your people,
     in the sanctuary of your Temple in
          Jerusalem,
     I will give you what I have promised.

Praise the LORD!

In Praise of the LORD

117 Praise the LORD, all nations!
          Praise him, all peoples!
²His love for us is strong
     and his faithfulness is eternal.

Praise the LORD!

A Prayer of Thanks for Victory

118 Give thanks to the LORD,
          because he is good,
          and his love is eternal.
²Let the people of Israel say,
     'His love is eternal.'
³Let the priests of God say,
     'His love is eternal.'
⁴Let all who worship him say,
     'His love is eternal.'

⁵In my distress I called to the LORD;
     he answered me and set me free.
⁶The LORD is with me, I will not be afraid;
     what can anyone do to me?
⁷It is the LORD who helps me,
     and I will see my enemies defeated.
⁸It is better to trust in the LORD
     than to depend on man.
⁹It is better to trust in the LORD
     than to depend on human leaders.

'And so I walk in the presence of the LORD in the world of the living.' (Psalm 116.9)

¹⁰Many enemies were round me;
>   but I destroyed them by the power of the
>   LORD!
¹¹They were round me on every side;
>   but I destroyed them by the power of the
>   LORD!
¹²They swarmed round me like bees,
>   but they burnt out as quickly as a fire
>   among thorns;
>   by the power of the LORD I destroyed
>   them.
¹³I was fiercely attacked and was being
>   defeated,
>   but the LORD helped me.
¹⁴The LORD makes me powerful and strong;
>   he has saved me.

¹⁵Listen to the glad shouts of victory in the
>   tents of God's people:
>   'The LORD's mighty power has done it!
¹⁶   His power has brought us victory—
>   his mighty power in battle!'

¹⁷I will not die; instead, I will live
>   and proclaim what the LORD has done.
¹⁸He has punished me severely,
>   but he has not let me die.

... I will live
and proclaim what the LORD has done.

---

¹⁹Open to me the gates of the Temple;
>   I will go in and give thanks to the LORD!

²⁰This is the gate of the LORD;
>   only the righteous can come in.

²¹I praise you, LORD, because you heard me,
>   because you have given me victory.

²²The stone which the builders rejected as
>   worthless
>   turned out to be the most important of all.
²³This was done by the LORD;
>   what a wonderful sight it is!
²⁴This is the day of the LORD's victory;
>   let us be happy, let us celebrate!
²⁵Save us, LORD, save us!
>   Give us success, O LORD!

²⁶May God bless the one who comes in the
>   name of the LORD!
>   From the Temple of the LORD we bless you.
²⁷The LORD is God; he has been good to us.
> With branches in your hands, start the
>   festival
>   and march round the altar.

²⁸You are my God, and I give you thanks;
>   I will proclaim your greatness.

²⁹Give thanks to the LORD, because he is good,
>   and his love is eternal.

The Law of the LORD

119
Happy are those whose lives
>   are faultless,
>   who live according to the
>   law of the LORD.
²Happy are those who follow his commands,
>   who obey him with all their heart.
³They never do wrong;
>   they walk in the LORD's ways.
⁴LORD, you have given us your laws
>   and told us to obey them faithfully.
⁵How I hope that I shall be faithful
>   in keeping your instructions!
⁶If I pay attention to all your commands,
>   then I will not be put to shame.
⁷As I learn your righteous judgements,
>   I will praise you with a pure heart.
⁸I will obey your laws;
>   never abandon me!

Obedience to the Law of the LORD

⁹How can a young man keep his life pure?
>   By obeying your commands.
¹⁰With all my heart I try to serve you;
>   keep me from disobeying your
>   commandments.
¹¹I keep your law in my heart,
>   so that I will not sin against you.
¹²I praise you, O LORD;
>   teach me your ways.
¹³I will repeat aloud
>   all the laws you have given.
¹⁴I delight in following your commands
>   more than in having great wealth.
¹⁵I study your instructions;
>   I examine your teachings.

'Open my eyes, so that I may see the wonderful truths in your law.' (Psalm 119.18)

¹⁶I take pleasure in your laws;
　your commands I will not forget.

Happiness in the Law of the LORD

¹⁷Be good to me, your servant,
　so that I may live and obey your teachings.
¹⁸Open my eyes, so that I may see
　the wonderful truths in your law.

I take pleasure in your laws.

---

¹⁹I am here on earth for just a little while;
　do not hide your commands from me.
²⁰My heart aches with longing;
　I want to know your judgements at all
　　times.
²¹You reprimand the proud;
　cursed are those who disobey your
　　commands.
²²Free me from their insults and scorn,
　because I have kept your laws.
²³The rulers meet and plot against me,
　but I will study your teachings.
²⁴Your instructions give me pleasure;
　they are my advisers.

Determination to Obey the Law of the LORD

²⁵I lie defeated in the dust;
　revive me, as you have promised.
²⁶I confessed all I have done, and you
　answered me;
　teach me your ways.
²⁷Help me to understand your laws,
　and I will meditate on your wonderful
　　teachings.
²⁸I am overcome by sorrow;
　strengthen me, as you have promised.
²⁹Keep me from going the wrong way,
　and in your goodness teach me your law.

**Keep me from going
the wrong way ...**

---

³⁰I have chosen to be obedient;
　I have paid attention to your judgements.
³¹I have followed your instructions, LORD;
　don't let me be put to shame.
³²I will eagerly obey your commands,
　because you will give me more
　　understanding.

A Prayer for Understanding

³³Teach me, LORD, the meaning of your laws,
    and I will obey them at all times.
³⁴Explain your law to me, and I will obey it:
    I will keep it with all my heart.
³⁵Keep me obedient to your commandments,
    because in them I find happiness.
³⁶Give me the desire to obey your laws
    rather than to get rich.
³⁷Keep me from paying attention to what is
        worthless;
    be good to me, as you have promised.
³⁸Keep your promise to me, your servant—
    the promise you make to those who obey
        you.
³⁹Save me from the insults I fear;
    how wonderful are your judgements!
⁴⁰I want to obey your commands;
    give me new life, for you are righteous.

Trusting the Law of the LORD

⁴¹Show me how much you love me, LORD,
    and save me according to your promise.
⁴²Then I can answer those who insult me
    because I trust in your word.

... I trust in your word.

---

⁴³Enable me to speak the truth at all times,
    because my hope is in your judgements.
⁴⁴I will always obey your law,
    for ever and ever.
⁴⁵I will live in perfect freedom,
    because I try to obey your teachings.
⁴⁶I will announce your commands to kings
    and I will not be ashamed.
⁴⁷I find pleasure in obeying your commands,
    because I love them.
⁴⁸I respect and love your commandments;
    I will meditate on your instructions.

Confidence in the Law of the LORD

⁴⁹Remember your promise to me, your
        servant;
    it has given me hope.
⁵⁰Even in my suffering I was comforted
    because your promise gave me life.
⁵¹The proud are always scornful of me,
    but I have not departed from your law.

⁵²I remember your judgements of long ago,
    and they bring me comfort, O LORD.
⁵³When I see the wicked breaking your law,
    I am filled with anger.
⁵⁴During my brief earthly life
    I compose songs about your commands.
⁵⁵In the night I remember you, LORD,
    and I think about your law.
⁵⁶I find my happiness
    in obeying your commands.

Devotion to the Law of the LORD

⁵⁷You are all I want, O LORD;
    I promise to obey your laws.
⁵⁸I ask you with all my heart
    to have mercy on me, as you have
        promised!
⁵⁹I have considered my conduct,
    and I promise to follow your instructions.
⁶⁰Without delay I hurry
    to obey your commands.
⁶¹The wicked have laid a trap for me,
    but I do not forget your law.
⁶²In the middle of the night I wake up
    to praise you for your righteous
        judgements.
⁶³I am a friend of all who serve you,
    of all who obey your laws.
⁶⁴LORD, the earth is full of your constant love;
    teach me your commandments.

The Value of the Law of the LORD

⁶⁵You have kept your promise, LORD,
    and you are good to me, your servant.
⁶⁶Give me wisdom and knowledge,
    because I trust in your commands.

Give me wisdom and knowledge,
because I trust in your commands.

---

⁶⁷Before you punished me, I used to go wrong,
    but now I obey your word.
⁶⁸How good you are—how kind!
    Teach me your commands.
⁶⁹Proud men have told lies about me,
    but with all my heart I obey your
        instructions.
⁷⁰These men have no understanding,
    but I find pleasure in your law.

⁷¹My punishment was good for me,
    because it made me learn your commands.
⁷²The law that you gave means more to me
    than all the money in the world.

The Justice of the Law of the LORD

⁷³You created me, and you keep me safe;
    give me understanding, so that I may
    learn your laws.
⁷⁴Those who honour you will be glad when
    they see me,
    because I trust in your promise.
⁷⁵I know that your judgements are righteous,
    LORD,
    and that you punished me because you are
    faithful.

Let your constant love comfort me ...

---

⁷⁶Let your constant love comfort me,
    as you have promised me, your servant.
⁷⁷Have mercy on me, and I will live
    because I take pleasure in your law.
⁷⁸May the proud be ashamed for falsely
    accusing me;
    as for me, I will meditate on your
    instructions.
⁷⁹May those who honour you come to me—
    all those who know your commands.
⁸⁰May I perfectly obey your commandments
    and be spared the shame of defeat.

A Prayer for Deliverance

⁸¹I am worn out, LORD, waiting for you to save
    me;
    I place my trust in your word.
⁸²My eyes are tired from watching for what
    you promised,
    while I ask, 'When will you help me?'
⁸³I am as useless as a discarded wineskin;
    yet I have not forgotten your commands.
⁸⁴How much longer must I wait?
    When will you punish those who
    persecute me?
⁸⁵Proud men, who do not obey your law,
    have dug pits to trap me.
⁸⁶Your commandments are all trustworthy;
    men persecute me with lies—help me!
⁸⁷They have almost succeeded in killing me,

but I have not neglected your commands.
⁸⁸Because of your constant love be good to me,
    so that I may obey your laws.

Faith in the Law of the LORD

⁸⁹Your word, O LORD, will last for ever;
    it is eternal in heaven.
⁹⁰Your faithfulness endures through all the
    ages;
    you have set the earth in place, and it
    remains.
⁹¹All things remain to this day because of your
    command,
    because they are all your servants.
⁹²If your law had not been the source of my
    joy,
    I would have died from my sufferings.
⁹³I will never neglect your instructions,
    because by them you have kept me alive.
⁹⁴I am yours—save me!
    I have tried to obey your commands.
⁹⁵Wicked men are waiting to kill me,
    but I will meditate on your laws.
⁹⁶I have learnt that everything has limits;
    but your commandment is perfect.

'Your word, O LORD, ... is eternal in heaven.' (Psalm 119.89)

Love for the Law of the LORD

[97]How I love your law!
   I think about it all day long.
[98]Your commandment is with me all the time
   and makes me wiser than my enemies.
[99]I understand more than all my teachers,
   because I meditate on your instructions.
[100]I have greater wisdom than old men,
   because I obey your commands.
[101]I have avoided all evil conduct,
   because I want to obey your word.
[102]I have not neglected your instructions,
   for you yourself are my teacher.
[103]How sweet is the taste of your
      instructions—
   sweeter even than honey!
[104]I gain wisdom from your laws,
   and so I hate all bad conduct.

Light from the Law of the LORD

[105]Your word is a lamp to guide me
   and a light for my path.
[106]I will keep my solemn promise
   to obey your just instructions.
[107]My sufferings, LORD, are terrible indeed;
   keep me alive, as you have promised.

[108]Accept my prayer of thanks, O LORD,
   and teach me your commands.
[109]I am always ready to risk my life;
   I have not forgotten your law.

**Your word is a lamp to guide me
and a light for my path.**

---

[110]Wicked men lay a trap for me,
   but I have not disobeyed your commands.
[111]Your commandments are my eternal
      possession;
   they are the joy of my heart.
[112]I have decided to obey your laws
   until the day I die.

Safety in the Law of the LORD

[113]I hate those who are not completely loyal to
      you,
   but I love your law.
[114]You are my defender and protector;
   I put my hope in your promise.
[115]Go away from me, you sinful people.
   I will obey the commands of my God.

[116]Give me strength, as you promised, and I
    shall live;
  don't let me be disappointed in my hope!
[117]Hold me, and I will be safe,
    and I will always pay attention to your
    commands.
[118]You reject everyone who disobeys your laws;
    their deceitful schemes are useless.
[119]You treat all the wicked like rubbish,
    and so I love your instructions.
[120]Because of you I am afraid;
    I am filled with fear because of your
    judgements.

Obedience to the Law of the LORD
[121]I have done what is right and good;
    don't abandon me to my enemies!
[122]Promise that you will help your servant;
    don't let arrogant men oppress me!
[123]My eyes are tired from watching for your
    saving help,
  for the deliverance you promised.
[124]Treat me according to your constant love,
    and teach me your commands.
[125]I am your servant; give me understanding,
  so that I may know your teachings.

[126]LORD, it is time for you to act,
    because people are disobeying your law.
[127]I love your commands more than gold,
    more than the finest gold.
[128]And so I follow all your instructions;
    I hate all wrong ways.

Desire to Obey the Law of the LORD
[129]Your teachings are wonderful;
    I obey them with all my heart.
[130]The explanation of your teachings gives
    light
  and brings wisdom to the ignorant.
[131]In my desire for your commands
    I pant with open mouth.
[132]Turn to me and have mercy on me
    as you do on all those who love you.
[133]As you have promised, keep me from
    falling;
  don't let me be overcome by evil.
[134]Save me from those who oppress me,
    so that I may obey your commands.
[135]Bless me with your presence
    and teach me your laws.
[136]My tears pour down like a river,
    because people do not obey your law.

The Justice of the Law of the LORD

¹³⁷You are righteous, LORD,
      and your laws are just.
¹³⁸The rules that you have given
      are completely fair and right.
¹³⁹My anger burns in me like a fire,
      because my enemies disregard your
         commands.
¹⁴⁰How certain your promise is!
      How I love it!
¹⁴¹I am unimportant and despised,
      but I do not neglect your teachings.
¹⁴²Your righteousness will last for ever,
      and your law is always true.
¹⁴³I am filled with trouble and anxiety,
      but your commandments bring me joy.
¹⁴⁴Your instructions are always just;
      give me understanding, and I shall live.

A Prayer for Deliverance

¹⁴⁵With all my heart I call to you;
      answer me, LORD, and I will obey your
         commands!
¹⁴⁶I call to you;
      save me, and I will keep your laws.
¹⁴⁷Before sunrise I call to you for help;
      I place my hope in your promise.

**Before sunrise
I call to you for help;
I place my hope in your promise.**

---

¹⁴⁸All night long I lie awake,
      to meditate on your instructions.
¹⁴⁹Because your love is constant, hear me, O
      LORD;
      show your mercy, and preserve my life!
¹⁵⁰My cruel persecutors are coming closer,
      people who never keep your law.
¹⁵¹But you are near to me, LORD,
      and all your commands are permanent.
¹⁵²Long ago I learnt about your instructions;
      you make them to last for ever.

A Plea for Help

¹⁵³Look at my suffering, and save me,
      because I have not neglected your law.
¹⁵⁴Defend my cause, and set me free;
      save me, as you have promised.

¹⁵⁵The wicked will not be saved,
      for they do not obey your laws.
¹⁵⁶But your compassion, LORD, is great;
      show your mercy and save me!
¹⁵⁷I have many enemies and oppressors,
      but I do not fail to obey your laws.
¹⁵⁸When I look at those traitors, I am filled
         with disgust,
      because they do not keep your commands.
¹⁵⁹See how I love your instructions, LORD.
      Your love never changes, so save me!
¹⁶⁰The heart of your law is truth,
      and all your righteous judgements are
         eternal.

Dedication to the Law of the LORD

¹⁶¹Powerful men attack me unjustly,
      but I respect your law.
¹⁶²How happy I am because of your promises—
      as happy as someone who finds rich
         treasure.
¹⁶³I hate and detest all lies,
      but I love your law.
¹⁶⁴Seven times each day I thank you
      for your righteous judgements.
¹⁶⁵Those who love your law have perfect
         security,
      and there is nothing that can make them
         fall.
¹⁶⁶I wait for you to save me, LORD,
      and I do what you command.
¹⁶⁷I obey your teachings;
      I love them with all my heart.
¹⁶⁸I obey your commands and your
         instructions;
      you see everything I do.

A Prayer for Help

¹⁶⁹Let my cry for help reach you, LORD!
      Give me understanding, as you have
         promised.
¹⁷⁰Listen to my prayer,
      and save me according to your promise!
¹⁷¹I will always praise you,
      because you teach me your laws.
¹⁷²I will sing about your law,
      because your commands are just.
¹⁷³Always be ready to help me,
      because I follow your commands.
¹⁷⁴How I long for your saving help, O LORD!
      I find happiness in your law.

¹⁷⁵Give me life, so that I may praise you;
may your instructions help me.
¹⁷⁶I wander about like a lost sheep;
so come and look for me, your servant,
because I have not neglected your laws.

A Prayer for Help

120

When I was in trouble, I called
to the LORD,
and he answered me.
²Save me, LORD,
from liars and deceivers.

³You liars, what will God do to you?
How will he punish you?
⁴With a soldier's sharp arrows,
with red-hot charcoal!

⁵Living among you is as bad as living in
Meshech
or among the people of Kedar.
⁶I have lived too long
with people who hate peace!
⁷When I speak of peace,
they are for war.

The LORD Our Protector

121

I look to the mountains;
where will my help come
from?
²My help will come from the LORD,
who made heaven and earth.

³He will not let you fall;
your protector is always awake.

⁴The protector of Israel
never dozes or sleeps.
⁵The LORD will guard you;
he is by your side to protect you.

**The LORD will guard you;
he is by your side
to protect you.**

---

⁶The sun will not hurt you during the day,
nor the moon during the night.

⁷The LORD will protect you from all danger;
he will keep you safe.
⁸He will protect you as you come and go
now and for ever.

In Praise of Jerusalem

122

I was glad when they said to
me,
'Let us go to the LORD's
house.'
²And now we are here,
standing inside the gates of Jerusalem!

³Jerusalem is a city restored
in beautiful order and harmony.
⁴This is where the tribes come,
the tribes of Israel,
to give thanks to the LORD
according to his command.
⁵Here the kings of Israel
sat to judge their people.

⁶Pray for the peace of Jerusalem:
'May those who love you prosper.
⁷ May there be peace inside your walls
and safety in your palaces.'
⁸For the sake of my relatives and friends
I say to Jerusalem, 'Peace be with you!'
⁹For the sake of the house of the LORD our
God
I pray for your prosperity.

'I look to the mountains; where will my help come from?' (Psalm 121.1)

A Prayer for Mercy

123 LORD, I look up to you,
up to heaven, where you
rule.

²As a servant depends on his master,
as a maid depends on her mistress,
so we will keep looking to you, O LORD our
God,
until you have mercy on us.

³Be merciful to us, LORD, be merciful;
we have been treated with so much
contempt.
⁴We have been mocked too long by the rich
and scorned by proud oppressors.

God the Protector of His People

124 What if the LORD had not been
on our side?
Answer, O Israel!

²'If the LORD had not been on our side
when our enemies attacked us,
³then they would have swallowed us alive
in their furious anger against us;
⁴then the flood would have carried us away,
the water would have covered us,
⁵ the raging torrent would have drowned
us.'

⁶Let us thank the LORD,
who has not let our enemies destroy us.
⁷We have escaped like a bird from a hunter's
trap;
the trap is broken, and we are free!

**Our help comes from the LORD,
who made heaven and earth.**

⁸Our help comes from the LORD,
who made heaven and earth.

The Security of God's People

125 Those who trust in the LORD
are like Mount Zion,
which can never be shaken,
never be moved.

²As the mountains surround Jerusalem,
so the LORD surrounds his people
now and for ever.

³The wicked will not always rule over the land
of the righteous;
if they did, the righteous themselves
might do evil.
⁴LORD, do good to those who are good,
to those who obey your commands.
⁵But when you punish the wicked,
punish also those who abandon your
ways.

Peace be with Israel!

A Prayer for Deliverance

126 When the LORD brought us
back to Jerusalem,
it was like a dream!
²How we laughed, how we sang for joy!
Then the other nations said about us,
'The LORD did great things for them.'
³Indeed he did great things for us;
how happy we were!

⁴LORD, make us prosperous again,
just as the rain brings water back to dry
river-beds.
⁵Let those who wept as they sowed their seed,
gather the harvest with joy!

⁶Those who wept as they went out carrying
the seed
will come back singing for joy,
as they bring in the harvest.

In Praise of God's Goodness

127 If the LORD does not build the
house,
the work of the builders is
useless;
if the LORD does not protect the city,
it is useless for the sentries to stand
guard.
²It is useless to work so hard for a living,
getting up early and going to bed late.
For the LORD provides for those he loves,
while they are asleep.

³Children are a gift from the LORD;
   they are a real blessing.
⁴The sons a man has when he is young
   are like arrows in a soldier's hand.
⁵Happy is the man who has many such
     arrows.
 He will never be defeated
   when he meets his enemies in the place of
    judgement.

The Reward of Obedience to the LORD

128
Happy are those who obey the
   LORD,
   who live by his commands.

²Your work will provide for your needs;
   you will be happy and prosperous.
³Your wife will be like a fruitful vine in your
    home,
   and your sons will be like young olive-
    trees round your table.
⁴A man who obeys the LORD
   will surely be blessed like this.

⁵May the LORD bless you from Zion!
   May you see Jerusalem prosper
   all the days of your life!
⁶May you live to see your grandchildren!

Peace be with Israel!

A Prayer against Israel's Enemies

129
Israel, tell us how your
    enemies have
    persecuted you
ever since you were young.

²'Ever since I was young,
   my enemies have persecuted me cruelly,
   but they have not overcome me.
³They cut deep wounds in my back
   and made it like a ploughed field.
⁴But the LORD, the righteous one,
   has freed me from slavery.'

⁵May everyone who hates Zion
   be defeated and driven back.

'Children are a gift from the LORD.' (Psalm 127.3)

⁶May they all be like grass growing on the
house-tops,
which dries up before it can grow;
⁷ no one gathers it up
or carries it away in bundles.
⁸No one who passes by will say,
'May the LORD bless you!
We bless you in the name of the LORD.'

A Prayer for Help

130
From the depths of my
despair I call to you,
LORD.
²Hear my cry, O Lord;
listen to my call for help!
³If you kept a record of our sins,
who could escape being condemned?
⁴But you forgive us,
so that we should stand in awe of you.

⁵I wait eagerly for the LORD's help,
and in his word I trust.
⁶I wait for the Lord
more eagerly than watchmen wait for the
dawn—
than watchmen wait for the dawn.

⁷Israel, trust in the LORD,
because his love is constant
and he is always willing to save.
⁸He will save his people Israel
from all their sins.

A Prayer of Humble Trust

131
LORD, I have given up my pride
and turned away from my
arrogance.
I am not concerned with great matters
or with subjects too difficult for me.

... my heart is quiet within me.

---

²Instead, I am content and at peace.
As a child lies quietly in its mother's arms,
so my heart is quiet within me.
³Israel, trust in the LORD
now and for ever!

In Praise of the Temple

132
LORD, do not forget David
and all the hardships he
endured.
²Remember, LORD, what he promised,
the vow he made to you, the Mighty God
of Jacob:
³'I will not go home or go to bed;
⁴ I will not rest or sleep,
⁵ until I provide a place for the LORD,
a home for the Mighty God of Jacob.'

⁶In Bethlehem we heard about the Covenant
Box,
and we found it in the fields of Jearim.

**'Let us go to the LORD's house;
let us worship
before his throne.'**

---

⁷We said, 'Let us go to the LORD's house;
let us worship before his throne.'

⁸Come to the Temple, LORD, with the
Covenant Box,
the symbol of your power,
and stay here for ever.
⁹May your priests do always what is right;
may your people shout for joy!

¹⁰You made a promise to your servant David;
do not reject your chosen king, LORD.
¹¹You made a solemn promise to David—
a promise you will not take back:
'I will make one of your sons king,
and he will rule after you.
¹²If your sons are true to my covenant
and to the commands I give them,
their sons, also, will succeed you for all
time as kings.'

¹³The LORD has chosen Zion;
he wants to make it his home:
¹⁴'This is where I will live for ever;
this is where I want to rule.
¹⁵I will richly provide Zion with all she needs;
I will satisfy her poor with food.
¹⁶I will bless her priests in all they do,
and her people will sing and shout for joy.

'... I am content and at peace.' (Psalm 131.2) ▷

17Here I will make one of David's descendants
  a great king;
    here I will preserve the rule of my chosen
      king.
18I will cover his enemies with shame,
    but his kingdom will prosper and flourish.'

In Praise of Brotherly Love

133
How wonderful it is, how
  pleasant,
    for God's people to live
      together in harmony!
2It is like the precious anointing oil
    running down from Aaron's head and
      beard,
    down to the collar of his robes.
3It is like the dew on Mount Hermon,
    falling on the hills of Zion.
That is where the LORD has promised his
    blessing—
    life that never ends.

A Call to Praise God

134
Come, praise the LORD,
    all his servants,
    all who serve in his
      Temple at night.
2Raise your hands in prayer in the Temple,
    and praise the LORD!

3May the LORD, who made heaven and earth,
    bless you from Zion!

A Hymn of Praise

135
Praise the LORD!

Praise his name, you
    servants of the LORD,
2 who stand in the LORD's house,
    in the Temple of our God.

3Praise the LORD, because he is good;
    sing praises to his name, because he is
      kind.
4He chose Jacob for himself,
    the people of Israel for his own.

5I know that our LORD is great,
    greater than all the gods.
6He does whatever he wishes
    in heaven and on earth,
    in the seas and in the depths below.
7He brings storm clouds from the ends of the
      earth;
    he makes lightning for the storms,
    and he brings out the wind from his
      storeroom.

8In Egypt he killed all the first-born
    of men and animals alike.
9There he performed miracles and wonders
    to punish the king and all his officials.
10He destroyed many nations
    and killed powerful kings:
11Sihon, king of the Amorites,
    Og, king of Bashan,
    and all the kings in Canaan.
12He gave their lands to his people;
    he gave them to Israel.

13LORD, you will always be proclaimed as God;
    all generations will remember you.
14The LORD will defend his people;
    he will take pity on his servants.

¹⁵The gods of the nations are made of silver
      and gold;
   they are formed by human hands.
¹⁶They have mouths, but cannot speak,
   and eyes, but cannot see.
¹⁷They have ears, but cannot hear;
   they are not even able to breathe.
¹⁸May all who made them and who trust in
      them
   become like the idols they have made!

¹⁹Praise the LORD, people of Israel;
   praise him, you priests of God!
²⁰Praise the LORD, you Levites;
   praise him, all you that worship him!
²¹Praise the LORD in Zion,
   in Jerusalem, his home.

   Praise the LORD!

A Hymn of Thanksgiving

136 Give thanks to the LORD,
         because he is good;
         his love is eternal.
²Give thanks to the greatest of all gods;
   his love is eternal.
³Give thanks to the mightiest of all lords;
   his love is eternal.

⁴He alone performs great miracles;
   his love is eternal.
⁵By his wisdom he made the heavens;
   his love is eternal;

His love is eternal.

⁶he built the earth on the deep waters;
   his love is eternal.
⁷He made the sun and the moon;
   his love is eternal;
⁸the sun to rule over the day;
   his love is eternal;
⁹the moon and the stars to rule over the night;
   his love is eternal.

¹⁰He killed the first-born sons of the
      Egyptians;
   his love is eternal.

¹¹He led the people of Israel out of Egypt;
   his love is eternal;
¹²with his strong hand, his powerful arm;
   his love is eternal.
¹³He divided the Red Sea;
   his love is eternal;
¹⁴he led his people through it;
   his love is eternal;

Give thanks to the mightiest
of all lords.

¹⁵but he drowned the king of Egypt and his
      army;
   his love is eternal.

¹⁶He led his people through the desert;
   his love is eternal.
¹⁷He killed powerful kings;
   his love is eternal;
¹⁸he killed famous kings;
   his love is eternal;
¹⁹Sihon, king of the Amorites;
   his love is eternal;
²⁰and Og, king of Bashan;
   his love is eternal.
²¹He gave their lands to his people;
   his love is eternal;
²²he gave them to Israel, his servant;
   his love is eternal.

²³He did not forget us when we were defeated;
   his love is eternal;
²⁴he freed us from our enemies;
   his love is eternal.
²⁵He gives food to every living creature;
   his love is eternal.

²⁶Give thanks to the God of heaven;
   his love is eternal.

A Lament of Israelites in Exile

137 By the rivers of Babylon we
         sat down;
         there we wept when we
         remembered Zion.
²On the willows near by
   we hung up our harps.

'Even though you are so high above, you care for the lowly ...' (Psalm 138.6)

³Those who captured us told us to sing;
  they told us to entertain them:
  'Sing us a song about Zion.'

⁴How can we sing a song to the LORD
  in a foreign land?
⁵May I never be able to play the harp again
  if I forget you, Jerusalem!
⁶May I never be able to sing again
  if I do not remember you,
    if I do not think of you as my greatest
      joy!

⁷Remember, LORD, what the Edomites did
  the day Jerusalem was captured.
  Remember how they kept saying,
    'Tear it down to the ground!'

⁸Babylon, you will be destroyed.
  Happy is the man who pays you back
    for what you have done to us—
⁹ who takes your babies
    and smashes them against a rock.

A Prayer of Thanksgiving

138
I thank you, LORD, with all my
    heart;
  I sing praise to you before
    the gods.
²I face your holy Temple,
  bow down, and praise your name

because of your constant love and
    faithfulness,
  because you have shown that your name
    and your commands are supreme.
³You answered me when I called to you;
  with your strength you strengthened
    me.

⁴All the kings in the world will praise you,
    LORD,
  because they have heard your promises.

**You answered me
when I called to you;
with your strength
you strengthened me.**

---

⁵They will sing about what you have done
  and about your great glory.
⁶Even though you are so high above,
  you care for the lowly,
    and the proud cannot hide from you.

⁷When I am surrounded by troubles,
  you keep me safe.
  You oppose my angry enemies
    and save me by your power.
⁸You will do everything you have promised;
  LORD, your love is eternal.
  Complete the work that you have begun.

God's Complete Knowledge and Care

139

LORD, you have examined me
and you know me.
²You know everything I do;
from far away you understand all my
thoughts.
³You see me, whether I am working or
resting;
you know all my actions.
⁴Even before I speak,
you already know what I will say.
⁵You are all round me on every side;
you protect me with your power.

Where could I go
to escape from you?

---

⁶Your knowledge of me is too deep;
it is beyond my understanding.

⁷Where could I go to escape from you?
Where could I get away from your
presence?
⁸If I went up to heaven, you would be there;
if I lay down in the world of the dead, you
would be there.
⁹If I flew away beyond the east
or lived in the farthest place in the west,
¹⁰you would be there to lead me,
you would be there to help me.
¹¹I could ask the darkness to hide me
or the light round me to turn into night,
¹²but even darkness is not dark for you,
and the night is as bright as the day.
Darkness and light are the same to you.

¹³You created every part of me;
you put me together in my mother's
womb.
¹⁴I praise you because you are to be feared;
all you do is strange and wonderful.
I know it with all my heart.
¹⁵When my bones were being formed,
carefully put together in my mother's
womb,
when I was growing there in secret,
you knew that I was there—
¹⁶   you saw me before I was born.
The days allotted to me

had all been recorded in your book,
before any of them ever began.
¹⁷O God, how difficult I find your thoughts;
how many of them there are!
¹⁸If I counted them, they would be more than
the grains of sand.
When I awake, I am still with you.

¹⁹O God, how I wish you would kill the wicked!
How I wish violent men would leave me
alone!
²⁰They say wicked things about you;
they speak evil things against your name.
²¹O LORD, how I hate those who hate you!
How I despise those who rebel against
you!
²²I hate them with a total hatred;
I regard them as my enemies.

²³Examine me, O God, and know my mind;
test me, and discover my thoughts.

Find out if there is any evil in me
and guide me in the everlasting way.

---

²⁴Find out if there is any evil in me
and guide me in the everlasting way.

A Prayer for Protection

140

Save me, LORD, from evil men;
keep me safe from violent
men.
²They are always plotting evil,
always stirring up quarrels.
³Their tongues are like deadly snakes;
their words are like a cobra's poison.

⁴Protect me, LORD, from the power of the
wicked;
keep me safe from violent men
who plot my downfall.
⁵Proud men have set a trap for me;
they have laid their snares
and along the path they have set traps to
catch me.

⁶I say to the LORD, 'You are my God.'
Hear my cry for help, LORD!

⁷My Sovereign LORD, my strong defender,
    you have protected me in battle.
⁸LORD, don't give the wicked what they want;
    don't let their plots succeed.

⁹Don't let my enemies be victorious;
    make their threats against me fall back on
        them.
¹⁰May red-hot coals fall on them;
    may they be thrown into a pit and never
        get out.
¹¹May those who accuse others falsely not
        succeed;
    may evil overtake violent men and
        destroy them.

¹²LORD, I know that you defend the cause of
        the poor
    and the rights of the needy.
¹³The righteous will praise you indeed;
    they will live in your presence.

An Evening Prayer

141

I call to you, LORD; help me
    now!
    Listen to me when I call to
        you.
²Receive my prayer as incense,
    my uplifted hands as an evening sacrifice.

³LORD, place a guard at my mouth,
    a sentry at the door of my lips.

Keep me from wanting to do wrong ...

---

⁴Keep me from wanting to do wrong
    and from joining evil men in their
        wickedness.
    May I never take part in their feasts.

⁵A good man may punish me and rebuke me
        in kindness,
    but I will never accept honour from evil
        men,
    because I am always praying against their
        evil deeds.
⁶When their rulers are thrown down from
    rocky cliffs,

the people will admit that my words were
    true.
⁷Like wood that is split and chopped into bits,
    so their bones are scattered at the edge of
        the grave.

⁸But I keep trusting in you, my Sovereign
        LORD,
    I seek your protection;
    don't let me die!
⁹Protect me from the traps they have set for
        me,
    from the snares of those evildoers.
¹⁰May the wicked fall into their own traps
    while I go by unharmed.

'Receive my prayer as incense, my uplifted hands as an evening sacrifice.' (Psalm 141.2)

A Prayer for Help

142

I call to the LORD for help;
   I plead with him.
²I bring him all my
      complaints;
I tell him all my troubles.
³When I am ready to give up,
   he knows what I should do.
In the path where I walk,
   my enemies have hidden a trap for me.
⁴When I look beside me,
   I see that there is no one to help me,
   no one to protect me.
No one cares for me.

⁵LORD, I cry to you for help;
   you, LORD, are my protector;
   you are all I want in this life.
⁶Listen to my cry for help,
   for I am sunk in despair.
Save me from my enemies;
   they are too strong for me.
⁷Set me free from my distress;
   then in the assembly of your people I will
      praise you
   because of your goodness to me.

A Prayer for Help

143

LORD, hear my prayer!
In your righteousness listen
   to my plea;
answer me in your faithfulness!
²Don't put me, your servant, on trial;
   no one is innocent in your sight.

³My enemy has hunted me down
   and completely defeated me.
He has put me in a dark prison,
   and I am like those who died long ago.
⁴So I am ready to give up;
   I am in deep despair.

⁵I remember the days gone by;
   I think about all that you have done,
   I bring to mind all your deeds.
⁶I lift up my hands to you in prayer;
   like dry ground my soul is thirsty for you.

⁷Answer me now, LORD!
   I have lost all hope.

Don't hide yourself from me,
   or I will be among those who go down to
      the world of the dead.
⁸Remind me each morning of your constant
      love,
   for I put my trust in you.
My prayers go up to you;
   show me the way I should go.

Show me the way I should go.

---

⁹I go to you for protection, LORD;
   rescue me from my enemies.
¹⁰You are my God;
   teach me to do your will.
Be good to me, and guide me on a safe path.

¹¹Rescue me, LORD, as you have promised;
   in your goodness save me from my
      troubles!
¹²Because of your love for me, kill my enemies
   and destroy all my oppressors,
   for I am your servant.

A King Thanks God for Victory

144

Praise the LORD, my protector!
He trains me for battle
   and prepares me for war.
²He is my protector and defender,
   my shelter and saviour,
   in whom I trust for safety.
He subdues the nations under me.

³LORD, what is man, that you notice him;
   mere man, that you pay attention to him?
⁴He is like a puff of wind;
   his days are like a passing shadow.

⁵O LORD, tear the sky apart and come down;
   touch the mountains, and they will pour
      out smoke.
⁶Send flashes of lightning and scatter your
      enemies;
   shoot your arrows and send them
      running.
⁷Reach down from above,
   pull me out of the deep water, and rescue
      me;

'Remind me each morning of your constant love ...' (Psalm 143.8)

save me from the power of foreigners,
8   who never tell the truth
    and lie even under oath.

⁹I will sing you a new song, O God;
    I will play the harp and sing to you.
¹⁰You give victory to kings
    and rescue your servant David.
¹¹Save me from my cruel enemies;
    rescue me from the power of
        foreigners,
    who never tell the truth
    and lie even under oath.

¹²May our sons in their youth
    be like plants that grow up strong.
May our daughters be like stately pillars
    which adorn the corners of a palace.
¹³May our barns be filled
    with crops of every kind.
May the sheep in our fields
    bear young by the tens of thousands.
¹⁴May our cattle reproduce plentifully
    without miscarriage or loss.
May there be no cries of distress in our
    streets.

¹⁵Happy is the nation of whom this is true;
    happy are the people whose God is the
        LORD!

A Hymn of Praise

145

I will proclaim your greatness,
    my God and king;
I will thank you for ever
    and ever.
²Every day I will thank you;
    I will praise you for ever and ever.
³The LORD is great and is to be highly praised;
    his greatness is beyond understanding.

⁴What you have done will be praised from
    one generation to the next;
    they will proclaim your mighty acts.

**The LORD is loving and merciful,
slow to become angry
and full of constant love.**

---

⁵They will speak of your glory and majesty,
    and I will meditate on your wonderful
        deeds.
⁶People will speak of your mighty deeds,
    and I will proclaim your greatness.
⁷They will tell about all your goodness
    and sing about your kindness.
⁸The LORD is loving and merciful,
    slow to become angry and full of constant
        love.

⁹He is good to everyone
and has compassion on all he made.

¹⁰All your creatures, Lord, will praise you,
and all your people will give you thanks.
¹¹They will speak of the glory of your royal
power
and tell of your might,
¹²so that everyone will know your mighty
deeds
and the glorious majesty of your kingdom.
¹³Your rule is eternal,
and you are king for ever.

The Lord is faithful to his promises,
and he is merciful in all his acts.
¹⁴He helps those who are in trouble;
he lifts those who have fallen.

¹⁵All living things look hopefully to you,
and you give them food when they need it.

All living things
look hopefully to you.

---

¹⁶You give them enough
and satisfy the needs of all.

¹⁷The Lord is righteous in all he does,
merciful in all his acts.
¹⁸He is near to those who call to him,
who call to him with sincerity.
¹⁹He supplies the needs of those who honour
him;
he hears their cries and saves them.
²⁰He protects everyone who loves him,
but he will destroy the wicked.

²¹I will always praise the Lord;
let all his creatures praise his holy name
for ever.

In Praise of God the Saviour

146 Praise the Lord!
Praise the Lord, my soul!
²I will praise him as long as I
live;
I will sing to my God all my life.

³Don't put your trust in human leaders;
no human being can save you.
⁴When they die, they return to the dust;
on that day all their plans come to an end.

⁵Happy is the man who has the God of Jacob
to help him
and who depends on the Lord his God,
⁶ the Creator of heaven, earth, and sea,
and all that is in them.
He always keeps his promises;
⁷ he judges in favour of the oppressed
and gives food to the hungry.

The Lord sets prisoners free
⁸ and gives sight to the blind.
He lifts those who have fallen;
he loves his righteous people.
⁹He protects the strangers who live in our land;
he helps widows and orphans,
but takes the wicked to their ruin.

¹⁰The Lord is king for ever.
Your God, O Zion, will reign for all time.

Praise the Lord!

In Praise of God the Almighty

147 Praise the Lord!
It is good to sing praise to
our God;
it is pleasant and right to praise him.
²The Lord is restoring Jerusalem;
he is bringing back the exiles.
³He heals the broken-hearted
and bandages their wounds.

⁴He has decided the number of the stars
and calls each one by name.
⁵Great and mighty is our Lord;
his wisdom cannot be measured.
⁶He raises the humble,
but crushes the wicked to the ground.

⁷Sing hymns of praise to the Lord;
play music on the harp to our God.
⁸He spreads clouds over the sky;
he provides rain for the earth
and makes grass grow on the hills.

⁹He gives animals their food
  and feeds the young ravens when they call.

¹⁰His pleasure is not in strong horses,
  nor his delight in brave soldiers;
¹¹but he takes pleasure in those who honour
    him,
  in those who trust in his constant love.

¹²Praise the LORD, O Jerusalem!
  Praise your God, O Zion!
¹³He keeps your gates strong;
  he blesses your people.
¹⁴He keeps your borders safe
  and satisfies you with the finest wheat.

¹⁵He gives a command to the earth,
  and what he says is quickly done.
¹⁶He spreads snow like a blanket
  and scatters frost like dust.
¹⁷He sends hail like gravel;
  no one can endure the cold he sends!
¹⁸Then he gives a command, and the ice melts;
  he sends the wind, and the water flows.

¹⁹He gives his message to his people,
  his instructions and laws to Israel.
²⁰He has not done this for other nations,
  they do not know his laws.

Praise the LORD!

A Call for the Universe to Praise God

148

Praise the LORD!

Praise the LORD from heaven,
  you that live in the heights above.
²Praise him, all his angels,
  all his heavenly armies.
³Praise him, sun and moon,
  praise him, shining stars.
⁴Praise him, highest heavens,
  and the waters above the sky.

⁵Let them all praise the name of the LORD!
 He commanded, and they were created;
⁶ by his command they were fixed in their
      places for ever,
  and they cannot disobey.

⁷Praise the LORD from the earth,
  sea-monsters and all ocean depths;
⁸lightning and hail, snow and clouds,
  strong winds that obey his command.

⁹Praise him, hills and mountains,
  fruit-trees and forests;
¹⁰all animals, tame and wild,
  reptiles and birds.

¹¹Praise him, kings and all peoples,
  princes and all other rulers;
¹²girls and young men,
  old people and children too.

**Praise him, kings and all peoples,
princes and all other rulers;
girls and young men,
old people and children too.**

¹³Let them all praise the name of the LORD!
 His name is greater than all others;
  his glory is above earth and heaven.
¹⁴He made his nation strong,
  so that all his people praise him—
  the people of Israel, so dear to him.

Praise the LORD!

'Praise him ... fruit-trees and forests.' (Psalm 148.9)

A Hymn of Praise

149

Praise the LORD!

Sing a new song to the LORD;
   praise him in the assembly of his faithful
      people!
2 Be glad, Israel, because of your Creator;
   rejoice, people of Zion, because of your
      king!
3 Praise his name with dancing;
   play drums and harps in praise of him.

4 The LORD takes pleasure in his people;
   he honours the humble with victory.
5 Let God's people rejoice in their triumph
   and sing joyfully all night long.

Praise the LORD!

---

6 Let them shout aloud as they praise God,
   with sharp swords in their hands
7   to defeat the nations
   and to punish the peoples;
8   to bind their kings in chains,
   their leaders in chains of iron;
9   to punish the nations as God has
     commanded.
This is the victory of God's people.

Praise the LORD!

Praise the LORD!

150

Praise the LORD!

Praise God in his Temple!
   Praise his strength in heaven!
2 Praise him for the mighty things he has done.
   Praise his supreme greatness.

3 Praise him with trumpets.
   Praise him with harps and lyres.
4 Praise him with drums and dancing.
   Praise him with harps and flutes.
5 Praise him with cymbals.
   Praise him with loud cymbals.
6 Praise the LORD, all living creatures!

Praise the LORD!

'Praise the LORD!' (Psalm 150.1)